WHAT TO BAKE

&

HOW TO BAKE IT

For me, baking is many things: a loving gesture, a way to pitch in or show support, or an invitation to a conversation. Sometimes it's just pure self-indulgence and the chance to step away from it all. I love baking because there's a recipe for every mood, occasion, and person I know; a favorite flavor, ingredient, or seasonal fruit. Baking is creative, scientific, a little bit magical, and a lot of fun. And, of course, homemade invariably tastes better than store-bought.

But what if you want to make a birthday cake and don't know where to begin? Or you've been asked to cook for a bake sale last minute? Or feel stuck with just a few recipes that you've tried and trusted? Here's where this book comes in: a compilation of favorite family baked goods, with something for every occasion and busy life, even if you've never baked before. If you're an experienced baker, there's plenty to discover and revisit. As a food writer and cooking teacher, I've been creating baking recipes for ten years now, but writing this book has taken me to new places—macarons, for instance, were something I usually bought rather than made. But now that I've worked out my way to make them simple, I'm hooked. And I've found ways to simplify and improve the most basic recipes, like jelly rolls or brownies, that I must have made 100 times before.

I've broken each recipe into several steps with all the detail a beginner needs. There's no substitute for actually being shown how to do something, so each step has a clear photo, and I've set out to make each recipe like a mini baking lesson; once you've cooked it, you'll want to bake it again, perhaps putting your own spin on it. New bakers will feel the confidence of a friendly voice behind each stir of the spoon.

The structure is designed with usefulness in mind too. The 50 recipes—mostly home-baking classics, with a few more adventurous ones—are grouped according to the occasion you might want to bake for. Simple Family Baking, which needs minimal bowls and time, is ideal for cooking with or for children; Morning Coffee & Afternoon Tea is a collection of easy-going treats for any time of day; Special Bakes covers classics for Christmas and other times when you want to make a special effort; and Desserts & After Dinner offers recipes suited to finishing a meal. Many include helpful tips, offer ways to take a shortcut, use a different pan, make ahead, or change flavors to suit you or the contents of the fridge better.

So many people tell me that they love cooking, but can't bake. I don't take that challenge lightly and always hear myself repeating the baking mantra: have patience, measure carefully, read the recipe before you begin, and it will do what it's supposed to. What I do recommend, if you are new to baking, is that you take time to read the next few pages carefully, especially the part about measuring. Together, this careful approach of words and pictures really works; readers tell me in letters and emails that the first two books in the *What to Cook* series have turned them (or their partners, children, friends, neighbors) from complete beginners into confident cooks with a good basic repertoire. I hope that this book will do the same for would-be bakers. It will help you discover (or rediscover) the joy of baking at home, and experience that unbeatably proud feeling: "I made that".

Happy baking,

Jane Hornby

How to Make the Recipes Work For You

It's my job to take the guesswork out of baking for you, and each recipe contains all the information you need to know. However, if you are a new baker, reading this section will arm you with the whys and wherefores behind the recipes. Here are the most important tips for getting the best out of them.

1
Make sure ingredients are at the correct temperature, especially butter and eggs.

2
Measure carefully and get all the ingredients out before you begin.

3
Don't make substitutions for ingredients or pans unless you absolutely have to.

4
Preheat the oven and grease and line any pans before you get started.

5
If a recipe contains baking soda or baking powder, always mix them with the other dry ingredients first before sifting.

6
Try to get cakes into the oven as soon as possible once the batter has been mixed together.

7
Use a timer to keep track of your baking, and try not to peek or open the oven too much to avoid losing heat.

8
Let cakes and other baked goods settle for a while in the pan or on their baking sheet before removing to a cooling rack.

Using measuring cups and spoons

If you read only one thing before you get started, make it this. Baking is simple, but an extra teaspoon here or different-size egg there really does make a difference to the end result, so it's important to measure accurately.

In the US, most ingredients are measured by volume in cups and spoons. Cups are less accurate than measuring the weight on a scale, so you'll need careful attention to get the best results. One standard American measuring cup holds 240 ml (or 8 fl oz, or 16 tablespoons). Buy a good-quality set of sturdy metal cups and measuring spoons from a reputable cookware shop. Unless stated otherwise, always fill the cup or spoon to the top and level it off. Use the right cup for each measurement, rather than measuring ½ cup in a 1-cup measure by eye, for example. For liquids, use a liquid measuring cup, which looks like a pitcher with measures on the side. It's best to use a 1-cup liquid cup for small measurements, as the markings are not as precise on larger cups.

To measure fine, dry ingredients such as flour and confectioners' sugar, use the fluff-spoon-sweep method. First, aerate it by fluffing and swirling it with a spoon or fork. Gently spoon heaped spoonfuls into the cup measure. Hold the cup over the package or a bowl to catch any excess. Keep going until the flour or sugar is mounded in the cup, and is at least as high as the edge of the cup all the way around. Take a straight-edged knife and lightly sweep away the excess. Don't pack or press the flour, or scoop it with the cup straight from the bag, as this compacts it into the cup. 1 cup flour measured this way is 4½ oz (125 g). For small amounts, just scoop from the bag with the measuring spoon, then level it off.

To measure regular white granulated sugars, spoon into the cup and level the top. They do not need the fluff-spoon-sweep method.

Dark and light brown sugars are measured packed. Spoon the sugar into the cup and press down with the back of the spoon to level the top of the cup. Don't pack it completely hard; a good, firm press is fine.

To measure butter, use the markings on the side of the stick wrapper to cut off the appropriate amount of tablespoons. One stick is 8 tablespoons, or ½ cup. Don't try and press it into a spoon measure.

For eggs, all the recipes call for large eggs, which weigh about 2 oz in their shells, and yield about 1¾ oz, or 3 tablespoons, once beaten. If you don't have the right egg size at hand, beat 1 more or 1 less egg, depending on the size you have, then measure the beaten amount, making sure you have 3 tablespoons beaten egg for every egg used in the recipe.

For thick or sticky liquids such as molasses, I find it helpful to very lightly oil the spoon or cup and the spoon I'm scooping from the jar with. This helps them flow out of the measuring cup or spoon and you get the right quantity in your recipe.

All other dry ingredients and thick liquids in this book have been spooned into the cups, not packed down, then leveled off.

Mastering Cakes

There are several methods for making cakes. The most common is the creaming method; a pound cake is a great example of this. Some, like gingerbread, are melting-method cakes, which are dense and moist. Some use the muffin method, in which the wet ingredients are stirred into the dry ones. Less common are rubbed-together mixes like scones, and whisked cakes, such as the light sponge of a jelly roll.

Creaming method
For this method, butter and sugar are beaten together thoroughly until pale and creamy looking, then eggs are added, followed by the other ingredients. You can do it by hand, but a stand mixer or handheld electric beaters will give the best results. I find that superfine sugar is quicker and easier to cream than granulated. For perfect cakes, the butter needs to be soft enough to spoon easily, but not so warm that it's greasy or melted (see page 18). Add the room-temperature eggs gradually; if the batter looks curdled or split when the eggs are going in (see page 18), add a little of the flour and it will become smooth again. Fold the flour and any liquid ingredients in carefully to preserve the air bubbles. Unless described otherwise, the batter should be "soft dropping consistency"—which means that a spoonful of batter should be soft enough to drop easily into the bowl when given a gentle shake.

I've made some of my creaming-method cakes using a speedier all-in-one method, in which the butter and sugar are first creamed, then everything else goes in the bowl at once and is beaten briefly to make a smooth batter. To take this shortcut yourself in other recipes, add 1 extra teaspoon baking powder to the dry ingredients, then follow as above.

Melting & muffin methods

Melting-method cakes are great for beginners, as the fat and sugar are simply melted together. Make sure they have cooled before adding the rest of the ingredients. These cakes tend to keep well. The muffin method simply involves mixing all the wet ingredients into the dry ones. To keep your cake light, try not to overmix or overbake it.

Rubbing-in method

This is a way of combining fat with flour, either by hand or in a processor, until they look like fine breadcrumbs, then liquid is added to make a dough. The butter must be cold and the dough must not be overmixed.

Whisking method

Whisked cakes can be the trickiest, and rely on the air beaten into the eggs to make them rise, rather than on rising agents like baking powder. Make sure the eggs are at room temperature and beat them with the sugar until very pale and thick. Fold in the dry ingredients very carefully to preserve the air.

Meringues

When making meringues, make sure the bowl and beaters are spotlessly clean. The term "stiff peaks" means that the beaten egg whites will hold their shape. Pull the beaters away from the bowl and hold them upright. If the whites fall or flop, they're not ready. If they point upwards or hold a stiff curve, they're ready. Don't add the sugar until this point, and be careful not to overwhisk them (see page 19). A meringue batter at stiff-peak stage with sugar added will be very thick and pearly, like shaving cream.

Pan sizes

For predictable baking, choose the correct size of pan for the recipe whenever you can. If you do have to substitute, remember that square pans have larger volumes than round ones, so use a square pan that's 1 inch smaller than its round equivalent, and vice versa. For other types of pan, measure the volume of your pan by pouring in cups of water and check that it's about the same as the pan specified in the recipe: a standard 8-inch round, 2-inch deep pan holds about 4 cups; a deeper 9-inch round springform pan holds about 10 cups; a 10-inch bundt pan 12 cups; a 9 x 13-inch rectangular pan 16 cups; a 9-inch square pan 7 cups, and a standard 8½ x 4½-inch loaf pan 4½ cups. If you're unsure, use a smaller pan and discard some of the batter rather than using a too-large pan. Never fill a pan more than two-thirds full, and check carefully that the cake is ready, as baking times may vary slightly.

Is it ready?

There are varying stages of readiness, depending on the recipe. Most cakes can be tested with a skewer, fine toothpick or, if you're really stuck, a strand of spaghetti. Insert it into the center; when you pull it out, a cooked cake will leave no trace, apart from a few damp crumbs or a little oiliness. If you see raw batter, it needs to go back into the oven as soon as possible. Test again in 5–10 minutes. If it wobbles or looks wet in the middle, don't test it yet; close the oven door carefully and check in 10–15 minutes. Some cakes can look cooked on the outside, but are still wet in the middle. In that case, cover it with a loose "hat" of foil, then continue to cook. The cake will not burn on the top before the center is done.

Other cues that tell you it's ready: the cake has risen all the way across the middle, possibly with cracks that look dry at the bottom. The sides will have shrunk away slightly from the pan and the cake will have an even golden color. Some things that we want to be gooey in the middle (like brownies) will jiggle instead. The surface should look set, but as you gently shake the pan you'll see a slight wobble under the surface. It won't look like liquid (that would be too undercooked), but rather like a set jelly.

Turning it out & letting it cool

Most cakes benefit from being left to cool in the pan for 10–15 minutes before transferring to a cooling rack. To remove a cake from a pan with a removable bottom, sit the pan on something narrow and tall, such as a jam jar. Press the pan down onto the jar, and the sides of the pan will slide down. Use an icing spatula or table knife to loosen between the lining paper and the pan. If the pan does not have removable sides or base, put something flat like a plate or board over it, then flip it upside down. Remove the pan, loosen the lining paper, then flip the cake onto a cooling rack. Take care if the top of the cake is delicate. Lift sheet cakes out by their lining paper. If the cake starts to sag a bit as you lift, get a helper to lift one side while you lift the other.

Perfect frosting

Making frosting is easy, but practice makes perfect when it comes to covering a cake like a pro; see the recipes on page 134 and 160 for advice. Bear in mind that icing often needs to be thicker than you think, so measure liquid ingredients carefully and add more confectioners' sugar if needed to thicken it up. Most cakes need to be completely cold before frosting or icing.

Cutting & serving

For sponge cakes, use a long, sharp serrated knife with a pointy end. Use a sharp non-serrated knife for firmer cakes like cheesecake and brownies. If your cake is frosted, wipe the knife on a paper towel before each cut. If splitting a cake in half to create layers, chilling it first can make a neater job. The key to cutting a large cake to serve a lot of people is to do it in a grid. Cut across the cake to give rectangular 2 x 1-inch slices (the offcuts are the chef's perk).

Storing & freezing cakes

To store baked goods in the cupboard, you can't beat an old-fashioned airtight metal cake tin. Always store them in a cool place, but only in the fridge if specified. If you want to get ahead, freezing cakes before frosting them (rather than storing them at room temperature) will keep them fresher, even for just a few days. Use sealable large freezer bags and plastic boxes and remove as much air as you can, and most will be fine in the freezer for up to 1 month. Defrost overnight, then frost or glaze. Most baked goods have the best flavor and texture when eaten at, or near, room temperature. If your cake is chilled, make sure you remove it from the fridge in good time.

What went wrong?

I hope none of the following things happens to your cakes, but there's always a reason for a cake not working properly, so you can fix it next time.

FLAT CAKE
Left too long before being put into the oven. Inadequate whisking or heavy-handed folding. Oven too cool. Old baking powder or baking soda.

OVERFLOWING CAKE
Pan too small, too much raising agent, too much liquid or not enough flour due to incorrect measuring.

SUNKEN CAKE
Removed from the oven too soon.

DRY OR OVERCOOKED CAKE
Oven too hot or baked for too long. Cake batter not "soft dropping consistency" (see page 8), if the recipe states it should have been.

CRACKED CAKE
Personally, I love some cakes with cracks in them, and I often design a recipe to have one on purpose! If your cake ends up cracked when you don't want it to be, it's normally due to the oven being too hot or the pan too small.

BIG BUBBLES OR HOLES
Insufficient mixing and sifting of rising agents into the flour. Batter left too long before going into the oven.

Mastering Pastry, Cookies & Bread

Pastry

There are three kinds of pastry in this book: basic pie dough or shortcrust, used for pies; choux paste, for profiteroles; and a rich, sweet pastry, which is perfect for delicate tarts and some cookies. You can of course buy ready-made dough and pie shells, but making most pastry is simple and quick, especially if you have a food processor. In general, light, flaky pastry needs cold butter and little handling for the best results. Basic pie dough always starts with cold butter and flour, which are rubbed together until they look like fine breadcrumbs. Very little liquid is then added to bring the dough together. It should feel dry to the touch, but should not crack or crumble. If you do need to add more liquid, add 1 teaspoon at a time and try not to overwork the dough as you add it. All pastry should be kept cool and rested before rolling it out. This helps prevent shrinking later and makes it easier to roll. If the dough starts being tricky to work with, chill it and try again.

Blind baking

This simply means baking the pastry twice before filling it, to avoid any sogginess or shrinkage. For the first bake, the cold pastry is lined with foil and held in place with pie weights (see page 14). These conduct the heat from the oven to the pastry, and help it to set in position. Without the foil and balls, the pastry would slip down the sides of the pan or bubble. The pastry is then baked again until cooked through. Pastry is dry and feels sandy when it's ready, and doesn't always need to be dark golden before it's done; it depends on the recipe. Basic pie crusts are very fragile when hot, and should be cooled in the pan. If you want to serve a tart or pie warm, just take it to the table in the pan.

Cookies

When making cookie doughs, try not to overwork the dough once the flour has been added, as this can make them tough. Measure rising agents accurately and leave plenty of room for them to spread on the baking sheets. They can burn easily so keep an eye on the cooking time. Always let them cool on a cooling rack before transferring to an airtight container.

Bread doughs

When strong bread flour and liquid are kneaded together, strands of gluten form, which give the bread its structure. Kneading it well (see page 69) is important to help the gluten develop. Don't be afraid of a wet or sticky dough; it will give you a better loaf. I use instant yeast for no-fuss baking, which can be added straight to the flour. Make sure your yeast is within the use-by date, and the liquid is not too hot. Find a warm, not drafty, place to let your dough rise, and cover it with oiled plastic wrap or a dish towel to prevent a skin forming. If you find it difficult to shape, let it rest for 5 minutes, then continue. The second rise, once the bread has been shaped, is called proofing. To check the proofing, gently press the side of the dough. If it doesn't spring back, it's ready to bake. Once baked, the base will be firm and sound hollow when tapped.

Freezing & storing other baked goods

Pastry, cookies, and bread are also ideal for the freezer and can be stored in the same way as cakes. Raw pastry can be chilled for 1 week or frozen for 1 month (shaped in its pan, if you like). Freeze small items flat on a baking sheet, then pack them into bags or boxes, layers interleaved with parchment paper and all air squeezed out. Refresh cooked bread and choux pastry in a hot oven for a few minutes. Store cooked pastry and cookies in airtight containers.

Equipment

Most of the recipes here are achievable by hand or machine, depending on your preference, and what equipment you are likely to have. Machines will certainly make many of them easier. See pages 14–17 for photographs.

Handheld electric mixers
I find these invaluable for baking, although most things can also be done with a good old wooden spoon or whisk. Handheld electric mixers save time, do a great job, and are more affordable than stand mixers.

Food processors & stand mixers
If you have a stand mixer, use it whenever you prefer for beating, whipping, and kneading. Food processors are great for making pastry, as they help work the dough together more quickly and use less liquid. They're also good for kneading dough using the plastic dough blade. Prep work, such as chopping nuts, is made faster, and rubbing in is transformed into a 1-minute job.

Ovens
There are two main kinds of oven: conventional and convection (or fan), and both can be electric or gas. Conventional ovens emit heat from the top and bottom, whereas convection ovens blow heat from the back. These have the benefit of cooking more evenly, although you may still need to move food around. The temperatures given in the recipes are for conventional ovens; follow the manufacturers' instructions to adjust cooking temperatures for convection ovens. A lower temperature is recommended for the latter, as the food will cook more quickly due to the effect of the hot circulating air. If you don't have the instructions for your oven, reduce the temperature by 25 degrees.

Oven thermostats are only accurate to a point, which is why it's best to be aware of what you are looking for as well as how long the recipe says it should cook for. Use a timer, plus the other sensory cues described on pages 9 and 11, and in the recipe, to decide if it's ready. Sometimes you'll need to turn a pan around as it cooks, especially if baking two things at once. Be quick, taking care not to let too much hot air out or cold air in. Get to know your oven, as sometimes the top or bottom shelves are hotter than the middle ones. Bake bread and pastry in the hottest part, and cakes and cookies in the middle.

Pans
Heavy, good-quality pans are best, and ideally with a pale finish. Darker pans can cause cakes and other baked goods to brown too much, and sometimes shorten cooking times a little. Most of the pans called for here are nonstick.

Preparing pans
Lining a pan is useful for two reasons: It helps you get the cake out of the pan and also acts as a layer of insulation, protecting the edges from overcooking. I mainly use butter to grease the pan before lining; just add enough to get the paper to stick. Nonstick vegetable oil spray is a quick alternative if you are short of time. Parchment paper is nonstick with a silicon coating, and is ideal for most recipes; do not use waxed paper, as it is not heat resistant. Re-usable silicon mats are a good choice and can be cut to size. Scones and breads can be baked using a little flour underneath instead. Muffins and cupcakes can go into their own paper liners or a greased nonstick pan.

Ingredients

Flour

Try to use good-quality unbleached flour, which has a more natural pale cream color, rather than bleached flour, which is very white and has been treated with chemicals. Adding rising agents such as baking powder or baking soda allows more control over how much each cake rises, so this is why I haven't used self-rising flour, which has rising agents already added. To make bread, you really do need to buy bread flour or unbleached high-protein all-purpose flour, but it's not necessary to buy cake flour for cakes. Instead, adding cornstarch to all-purpose flour softens the results, and you probably already have both in the cupboard. If you do want to use cake flour, use the total measure of all-purpose and cornstarch combined. Flours can vary in water content, which is why some doughs and batters may seem dry, even if you have followed the recipe exactly; you can always add a splash more liquid.

Gluten-free baking

If you prefer to substitute gluten-free flour for wheat flour, use a reputable brand and follow the instructions. You may also find xanthan gum useful.

Sugars & sweeteners

White superfine and granulated sugars are ideal for most cakes. I prefer superfine, as it creams together with butter more effectively, and also creates a finer crumb. Where a type of sugar is not specified, you can use granulated or superfine. Some people who want to cut down on sugar try to substitute honey or sweeteners for sugar when baking, but they are very different from sugar and will cause the recipe to behave differently. Golden syrup, such as Lyle's, is a British product with a unique flavor. If you can't find it, use light corn syrup instead. Don't subsitute honey or maple syrup; only golden or corn syrup has the stickiness you need.

Butter & oils

Unsalted butter is better for baking, and I don't recommend substituting margarine, which can really alter the balance of a recipe. Butter must be the right temperature for baking (usually soft and room temperature for cakes, but cold for pastry). Choose a flavorless oil for baking, such as canola.

Dairy products

When using yogurt and cream cheese, choose regular full-fat versions, and use whole milk. I use heavy cream for most cooking, although in some cases whipping cream is fine. Do not try to cook with light cream, as it will neither whip nor boil successfully. Sometimes I use milk and heavy cream together in a recipe in equal quantities; if you like, you can use "half and half" instead of the total volume. Use dairy products straight from the fridge.

Eggs

Use fresh, free-range, good-quality large eggs. If you have older eggs to use up, they will create a better meringue and are great for whisked cakes as they can whip up to a greater volume. Use eggs at the right temperature: room temperature for creamed-method and whisking cakes, cold for pastry.

Chocolate

I like to bake with bittersweet chocolate that contains 60% cocoa solids for most recipes, as this has a deep chocolate flavour but is easy to work with. 70% chocolate has an intense cocoa hit and works well for desserts and more decadent cakes. Take care when melting chocolate, as it can easily overheat and turn lumpy and unusable (see page 19); follow the instructions in the recipes carefully.

Citrus fruit

When using citrus fruits for zesting, either use organic, unwaxed fruit, or scrub well in soapy water before you start grating.

1

9-inch fluted tart pan: A pan with a removable bottom for tarts and pies with a delicate look, 1¼–1½ inches deep.

2

Wire cooling rack: A large, nonstick one is good; if you plan to bake a lot, you'll find it useful to have two.

3

Flat baking sheet: This has a lip on one side to hold on to, but the other edges are flat, making it easy to slide things on and off.

4

9-inch round springform cake pan: For cheesecakes, large dessert cakes that look elegant when cut into long, shallow slices, and large celebration cakes.

5

Pie weights: Ceramic balls that are essential for blind baking. You can also use dried pulses or rice, although they don't have such good heat-conducting properties.

6

9-inch pie pan: For classic deep-dish pies. Choose a metal one with a rim, as this will give you something for a crimped edge to stick to, and means you can add a lid, if you like.

7

8-inch round cake pans: Ideal for layer cakes that are quick to bake. Make sure yours are at least 2 inches deep, which will give cakes deep enough for cutting in half horizontally, and ideally with removable bottoms.

8

Deep 8-inch round cake pan: Ideal for Christmas and other fruit cakes.

1–3

4

5–6

7

8

1
Muffin pan and muffin liners
with deep wells.

2
Bundt pan: Creates a wonderfully
shaped cake. The central chimney
delivers heat to the center of the
cake, which speeds up cooking
and gives a very tender result.

3
9-inch square brownie pan: Perfect
for all sorts of bars and sliceable
baked goods.

4
Standard loaf pan: Measures 8½
x 4½ inches along the top inside
edges. I prefer one with sloping
sides, as straight edges mean the
pan is larger and cakes don't rise
into such a nice shape.

5
9 x 13-inch sheet cake pan: Perfect
for simple large bakes to cut into
squares or carve into a novelty
shape.

6
10 x 15-inch jelly roll pan: Wide
enough to use as a baking sheet
too.

7
Angel food cake pan: Straight-sided
and deep, this is probably the only
pan that cannot be substituted.

1

Food processor: For chopping and quick prep. This one has an 8-inch diameter bowl, 4½ inches deep, which is big enough to make cakes.

2

Mixing bowls of various sizes: You'll need at least one large bowl that is large enough to beat in and splash batter without it spilling over the edges. Pyrex bowls are ideal as they are heat resistant, can go in the microwave, and also stack neatly.

3

Large metal spoon for folding: The larger the spoon, the less folding you'll have to do, and the finer the metal, the more sharply it cuts through the batter.

4

Sieves: Choose one with a medium mesh for the large sieve, as it can be frustratingly slow sifting flour through a fine-mesh sieve. Make the mini sieve a fine one, for dusting sugar over finished recipes.

5

Rubber spatula: It should be flexible to help you scrape out the bowl, and a thin edge is good for folding.

6

Wooden spoon

7

Whisk: Metal is a more durable choice than plastic, although it can scratch some pans.

8

Handheld electric mixer: This is very handy, but you can also use a stand mixer.

1
Measuring spoons: 1 tablespoon, and ¼, ½, and 1 teaspoon.

2
Measuring cups: For dry goods and thick liquids. ¼, ⅓, ½, and 1 cup.

3
Weighing scale

4
Liquid measuring cups

5
Cookie cutters

6
Citrus fruit juicer

7
Skewer

8
Rolling pin: The straight part should be at least 12 inches long. Avoid those with a central spindle.

9
Ruler

10
Pastry bag and tips: Disposable bags are simple to use.

11
Bread knife or long serrated knife, plus small and large icing spatulas.

12
Pastry brush

13
Fine grater

14
Box grater

15
Peeler

16
Large ice-cream scoop

What to Look For

1

Softened butter: The butter should be soft but not greasy, so that it can easily be spooned or blended in a large bowl. If it seems too hard, warm it for just a couple of seconds in the microwave at medium power. Alternatively, cut it into small pieces and set it aside in a warm place. If it's too soft, put the bowl in the fridge or freezer for a few minutes and try again.

2

Creaming: The bowl on the left shows butter and sugar that have been beaten together, but not to the right extent.

The bowl on the right shows the correct creamy, very pale mixture, which has increased quite a bit in volume and changed from yellow to almost white.

3

Split batter: The bowl on the left shows creamed butter and sugar to which the egg has been added rather too quickly. The mixture has split, and looks curdled, lumpy, or slimy. This is the point at which you will need to add 1 tablespoon flour; adding more egg will make things worse, and a split batter can lead to a poor rise.

The bowl on the right has not split, and is light and fluffy.

4

Overwhisked egg whites: The bowl on the left shows egg whites before adding any sugar, which have been overbeaten. They look dry and have started to break up at the edges. There's not much of a fix for this, so take care while you whisk.

The bowl on the right shows the time to stop whisking and start adding sugar to make meringues; it is thick and stiff, but not dry.

5

Whipped cream: The bowl on the left shows cream that has been overwhipped and is turning thick and lumpy. This won't spread well and can be very hard to fold into other ingredients.

The bowl on the right shows perfectly whipped cream, soft and thickened. Cream thickens while it stands and as you pipe or spread it, so it's always best to under-whip it.

6

Overcooked chocolate: This shows burnt chocolate, which has turned thick and granular. Take care to melt chocolate carefully, as once it's like this, it can't be used.

SIMPLE
FAMILY BAKING

Golden Citrus Drizzle Cake

Preparation time: 15 minutes
Baking time: 35 minutes
Makes 12 large squares,
or more fingers

In my experience, a citrus drizzle cake always disappears first from the table at a fête or bake sale, so I've re-created it as a sheet cake that's easy to make, slice, and transport. Cornmeal or polenta adds a golden glow to the inside, but if you prefer you can substitute the same amount of all-purpose flour.

For the cake

2 sticks (1 cup) soft butter,
   plus extra for greasing
2 lemons
2 limes
1 mandarin or clementine,
   with a vibrant orange skin
1 cup sugar
4 eggs, room temperature
1 cup all-purpose flour
1 cup fine yellow cornmeal,
   or ½ cup plus 2 tbsp quick-
   cooking polenta
¼ tsp salt
2 tsp baking powder
½ cup lemon-flavored or plain
   whole yogurt

For the topping
½ cup granulated sugar

1
Preheat the oven to 350°F. Grease a 9-inch square pan with a little butter, then line the pan with parchment paper. Finely grate the zest from all the fruit, taking care not to remove the bitter white pith just underneath the colorful outer layer. Put 2 teaspoons of the mixed zests in a large bowl with the butter and sugar, saving the rest for later.

LOVE LEMONS? LIME-AHOLIC?
For a straight-up lemon cake or lime cake, simply use the zest and juice from one kind of fruit (you'll need 4 teaspoons zest and ⅓ cup juice). I find all orange a little too sweet for a drizzle cake, so add a little lemon juice and zest for extra bite.

2
Using an electric mixer, beat the butter and sugar together until creamy and pale. Scrape the sides of the bowl down every now and again with a spatula, so that every last bit gets mixed.

3
Crack the eggs into a liquid measuring cup (I do this because they plop from it individually, which is easier than stopping the beaters to crack an egg every now and again). Pour one egg into the bowl, then beat it into the creamed mixture until completely combined, fluffy, and light. Add the rest of the eggs one by one, beating well each time. If the mixture starts to look at all slimy, add 1 tablespoon of the flour and it will become smooth again.

MAKE IT BIGGER
To make a larger sheet cake, grease and line a 9 x 13-inch sheet cake pan and double the quantities. Bake at 350°F for 25 minutes, then at 325°F for another 25 minutes, or until a skewer comes out clean. Double the drizzle quantities too.

4

Thoroughly mix together the flour, cornmeal or polenta, salt, and baking powder, then sift half of it on top of the egg mixture. Using a spatula or a large metal spoon, fold it in until the batter is thick and fairly smooth.

5

Fold in the yogurt in the same way, then sift over and fold in the remaining dry ingredients. Scrape the batter into the prepared pan, level the top, then give the cake a sharp tap on the work surface to help remove any bubbles that can sometimes appear in this cake. Bake for 20 minutes, or until it is golden and has risen all over, then turn the oven down to 325°F. If it's browning too much on one side, quickly and carefully turn it around. Bake for another 15 minutes, or until firm to the touch, or it passes the skewer test (see page 32). Let cool in the pan on a wire rack for a few minutes.

6

Meanwhile, squeeze the juice from 1 lemon, 1 lime, and half the orange, to make about ⅓ cup. Poke 20 or so holes all over the cake using a fine skewer or a toothpick. Mix the granulated sugar into the juice (do not let it dissolve), then spoon it over the surface of the still-warm cake, making sure that the sugar looks thick and evenly spread.

7

Let cool completely. The sugar will become crisp and sparkly once the syrup soaks into the cake. Cut into squares to serve. If making the cake a day ahead, leave it loosely covered or in a roomy container with a little air for breathing. This will keep the sugary crust crisp.

Fruity Cupcakes

Preparation time: 10 minutes
Baking time: 18–20 minutes
Makes 12 regular or 36 mini cupcakes

All kids love to make cupcakes, right? But the eating (for this grownup, anyway) doesn't always quite live up to the excitement, so that's why this recipe is generous with the milk to make a fluffy cake with no hint of dryness about it. The fruit glaze is easily swapped for one of the other quick frostings in the book, if you prefer.

For the cakes

1 stick (½ cup) soft butter

¾ cup sugar, preferably superfine

1½ cups all-purpose flour

1 tbsp cornstarch

1½ tsp baking powder

¼ tsp salt

2 eggs, room temperature

½ tsp vanilla extract or paste

½ cup milk

For the fruity glaze

1–1¼ cups confectioners' sugar

½ cup mixed berries (fresh
  or frozen and defrosted)
  or 2 large, ripe passion fruit

1
Preheat the oven to 350°F. Line a muffin pan with 12 paper cupcake liners. Beat the butter and sugar together until pale and creamy. You can do this with a handheld electric mixer, but a wooden spoon is fine if you are cooking with children.

2
In another smaller bowl, mix together the flour, cornstarch, baking powder, and salt, then sift half of this mixture on top of the creamed butter and sugar. Add the eggs, vanilla, and half the milk too.

3
Beat the ingredients together, starting slowly at first, and keep going until creamy and smooth. In separate additions, add the rest of the flour mixture and then the milk, beating after each, to make a very soft batter. Don't worry if it looks a little separated once all the milk is in. Spoon the batter into the prepared pan, aiming for an equal amount in each paper liner.

MAKING SMALLER CAKES
If you prefer, this batter also makes 36 mini cupcakes, perfect for kids' parties. Line a 24-cup mini muffin pan with mini muffin liners. Fill the cases three-quarters full and bake for 13–15 minutes. Repeat with the remaining batter and 12 liners.

4

Bake for 18–20 minutes, or until the cakes have risen and are golden, and a skewer inserted into one of the central cakes comes out clean. Cool in the pan for 5 minutes, then transfer to a rack. If they start to brown unevenly during cooking, turn the pan around in the oven and continue to bake.

5

To make a berry glaze, use the back of a fork to crush the berries until juicy and well mashed. Sift the confectioners' sugar into the bowl, then stir to combine. For a passion fruit glaze, scoop the seeds and pulp from the fruit (you'll need about 4 tablespoons) and mix with the sifted confectioners' sugar. If either icing seems too runny, add a little more sugar (it will depend on the individual fruits and how juicy they are). Spoon the glaze over the cooled cakes and let set.

6

The cakes are best enjoyed as soon as the glaze has set, or can be kept in an airtight container for a couple of days. Un-iced cakes can be frozen for up to 1 month, then decorated once defrosted.

BUTTERFLY CAKES
To make this English teatime classic, use a small serrated knife to cut the tops off the cakes, then cut each top in half to make two semi-circles. Make the buttercream frosting on page 46. Spoon a generous dollop of buttercream on top of each of the cakes, then poke the "wings" pointing upwards into the cream, golden side up, with the curved edges facing away from each other. Add a little dot of jam, lemon curd or some sprinkles, and dust with confectioners' sugar to serve. You could also use sweetened whipped cream.

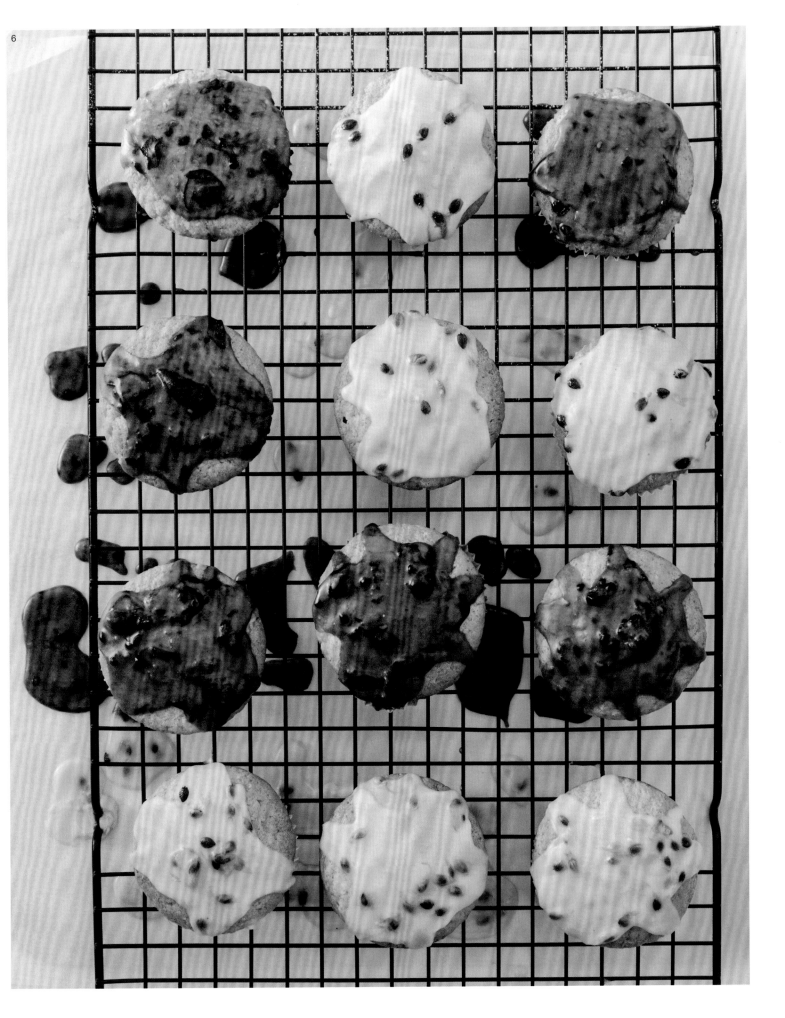

Buttermilk Pound Cake

Preparation time: 15 minutes
Baking time: 50–55 minutes
Cuts into 8–10 slices

Pound cake isn't fancy or smart, but has a reliable, rustic beauty. Served just as it is, or as a dessert with soft fruit and a dollop of cream, or perhaps covered with thick, lemony icing dripping down the sides for coffee time, this cake seems to fit any occasion. For flavor variations, turn to page 32.

1½ sticks (¾ cup) soft butter, plus extra for greasing
¾ cup plus 2 tbsp sugar
3 eggs, room temperature
1 tsp vanilla extract
1¾ cups all-purpose flour
½ tsp baking soda
½ tsp baking powder
¼ tsp salt
½ cup buttermilk (or see Tip)
1 tbsp confectioners' sugar (optional)

1

2

3

1

Grease an 8½ x 4½-inch loaf pan with a little butter, then line it with parchment paper. Cut a long, thin strip for the length of the pan, then another to go across the width, leaving some overhang on each side to make it easy to lift out the cake later. Preheat the oven to 350°F. Using an electric mixer, beat the butter and sugar together until very creamy and pale. Scrape the sides of the bowl down every now and again with a spatula, so that every last bit gets mixed.

2

Crack the eggs into a measuring cup and beat well with a fork. Pour about 2 tablespoons egg into the butter mixture, then beat until the egg is incorporated and the mixture becomes light and fluffy. Repeat, adding a little egg at a time, until all of the egg has been worked in. If the mixture starts to look at all slimy or lumpy, add 1 tablespoon of the flour and it will become smooth again. Beat in the vanilla extract.

3

Stir together the flour, baking soda, baking powder, and salt. Sift half of it on top of the beaten egg mixture, then fold in with a large metal spoon or spatula. Fold in the buttermilk, then repeat with remaining flour mixture to make a smooth, thick batter.

NO BUTTERMILK?
This cake can be made with milk instead. Measure ½ cup milk, then replace 2 tablespoons of it with lemon juice. Let stand for a few minutes until thickened, then use as above.

4
Scrape the batter into the pan,
then gently level the top.

5
Bake for 30 minutes, or until it has
risen and cracked in the center, then
turn the oven down to 325°F and
cook for 20–25 minutes more, until
a skewer comes out clean. Let the
cake cool in the pan for 15 minutes,
then remove it from the pan using
the lining paper to help. Let cool
completely on a wire rack.

THE SKEWER TEST
When any kind of sponge cake
is ready, a skewer or toothpick
inserted into the center will come
out clean (possibly a little greasy-
looking), or with a few damp crumbs
attached. If it has raw cake batter on
the end, the cake is not ready and
should be baked for 5–10 minutes
longer before testing again.

6
Once cooled, peel off the parchment
paper. Sift the confectioners' sugar
over the top, or try one of the ideas
below. This is at its best on the day
of baking, but will keep in an airtight
container, or can be frozen (without
icing, if using) for up to 1 month.

LEMON CAKE
Add the zest of 1 lemon and ½
teaspoon vanilla extract in step 2.
Stir 3½ teaspoons lemon juice into
1 cup sifted confectioners' sugar
until smooth, spoon it all over the
cooled cake, then let set.

STICKY MARMALADE CAKE
Use orange zest in the batter. Warm
4 tablespoons marmalade with
1 tablespoon citrus juice or water
and brush it over the warm cake.

CLASSIC ENGLISH SEED CAKE
Toast 1 teaspoon caraway seeds in
a hot dry pan to release the aroma.
Fold them in and bake as before.

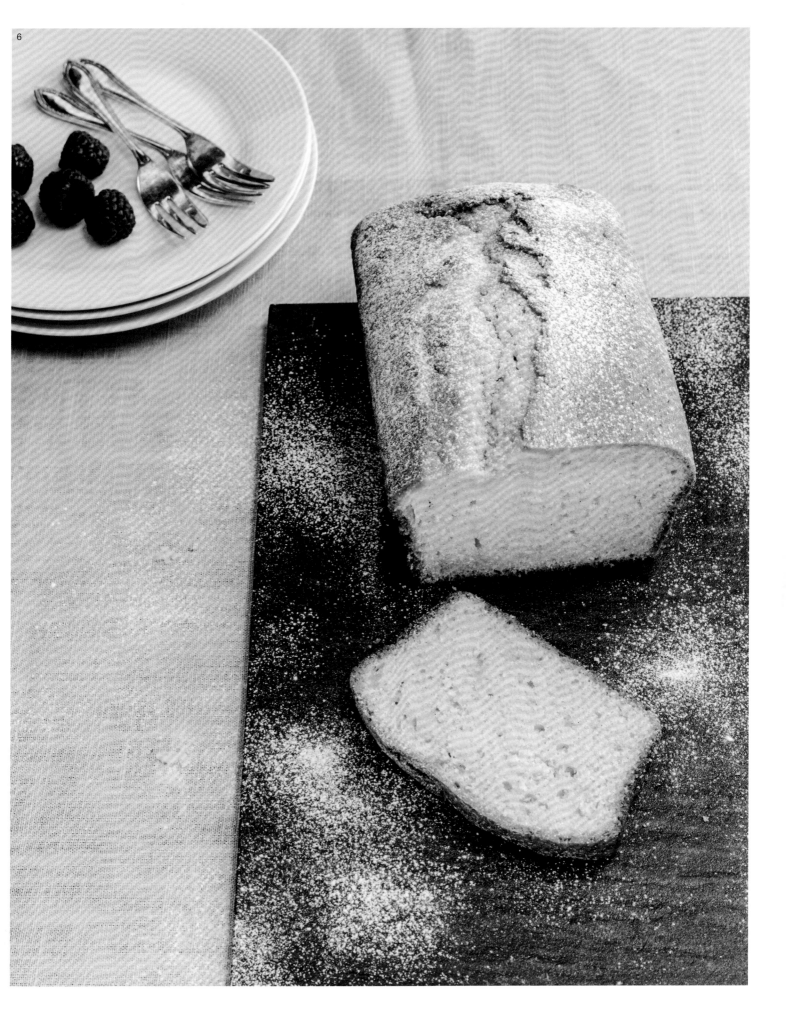

Peanut Butter Cookies

Preparation time: 15 minutes
Baking time: 10–12 minutes per batch
Makes 24

These have everything I look for
in a peanut butter cookie: a slightly
soft inside, a crisp outside, and
a salty sweetness that means one is
never enough. Like most homemade
cookies, they are best eaten on the
day of baking—no real hardship
there! There's a freeze-ahead option
if you prefer; see over the page.

---

1 cup whole unsalted roasted
    peanuts
2 cups all-purpose flour
½ tsp baking powder
⅓ packed cup light brown sugar
⅓ cup sugar
½ tsp salt
1¼ sticks (½ cup plus 2 tbsp) butter,
    room temperature
⅓ cup plus 1 tbsp smooth
    peanut butter
1 egg
2 tbsp honey

1
Preheat the oven to 350°F. Spread the nuts over a baking sheet and cook for about 8 minutes, or until pale golden. This step isn't essential if you're in a hurry, but it adds an extra deep, nutty flavor.

CAN'T FIND UNSALTED PEANUTS? You could also use salted roasted nuts (the snacking kind) for this recipe. Skip straight to step 2 and add only a pinch of salt to the dough instead of ½ teaspoon.

2
Chop the nuts with a knife, or use a food processor. I prefer mine quite chunky, but go as fine as you like.

3
Put the flour, baking powder, sugars, and salt in a large bowl and mix together. Cut the butter into cubes and add it to the bowl with the peanut butter.

4

Rub the peanut butter and butter into the dry ingredients using your fingers and thumbs. To do this, use both hands to lift some of the butter, peanut butter and flour from the bowl. Gently pinch the butters and flour together as they pass through your fingers back into the bowl. Keep going, and eventually you will have a mixture that looks like fine crumbs. You can do this with a food processor, if you prefer. Beat the egg. Add two-thirds of the chopped toasted peanuts to the mixture, then the egg and honey.

5

Mix everything together with a table knife or wooden spoon to make a rough, fairly sticky dough. Try not to overwork it, as this can make your cookies tough.

MAKE AHEAD
You can shape the dough into 2 logs about 3 inches across, roll each one in the nuts (chopped a little finer), then wrap tightly in plastic wrap and chill or freeze. Slice and bake the cookies as you need them.

6

Line 2 flat baking sheets with parchment paper. Pinch off a walnut-size ball of dough and roll it between your palms until smooth. Press the ball into the chopped nuts, squishing it to a flatter disk. Place nut-side up on the baking sheet, then repeat. Leave plenty of space between the cookies.

7

Bake for 10–12 minutes (about 13 minutes from frozen), or until evenly golden. Roll and squash the next batch of cookies while the first batch bakes. Let them cool on the baking sheets for a few minutes before transferring to a rack to cool completely. Store in an airtight container and eat within 3 days.

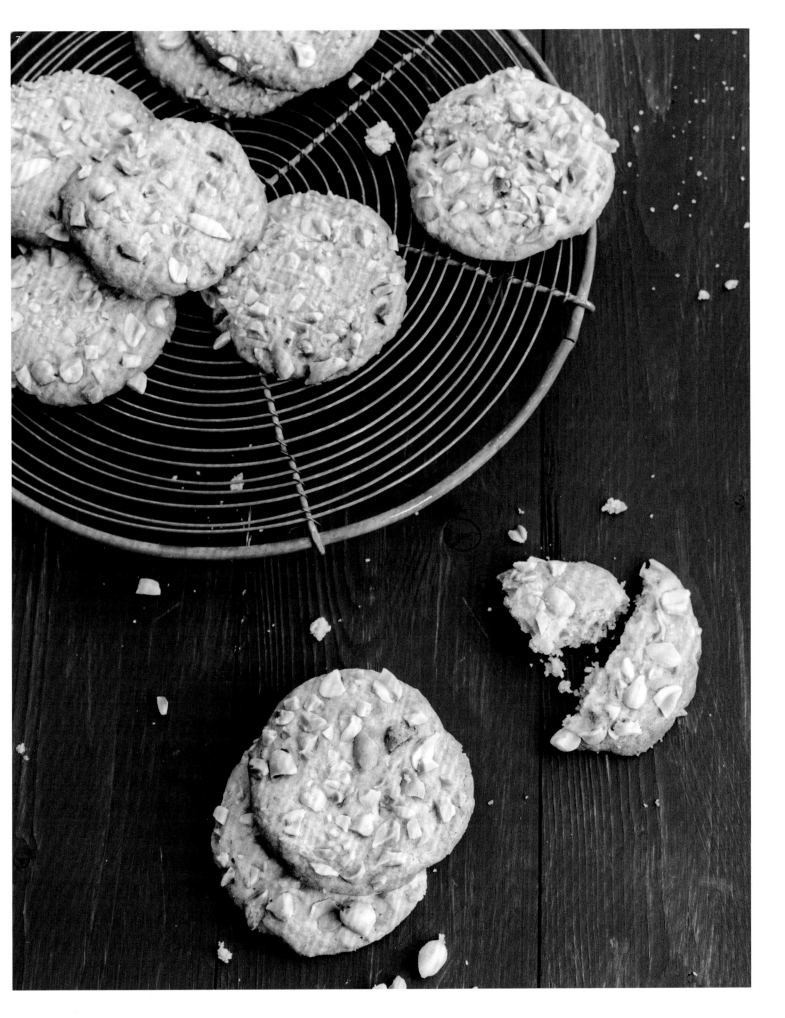

Favorite Jelly Roll

Preparation time: 15 minutes
Baking time: 10 minutes
Makes 10 slices

A jelly roll was one of the first things I ever baked with my mom, probably because it was so quick to make, and all the ingredients were in the pantry. Although there are lots of steps, be assured that it's a simple cake, and one of the most popular among friends and family when I was creating the recipes for this book.

For the cake
½ stick (¼ cup) butter, plus extra
    for greasing
3 tbsp milk
4 eggs, room temperature
¾ cup sugar, preferably superfine
1 tbsp cornstarch
1 cup all-purpose flour
¼ tsp salt

For rolling and filling
¼ cup sugar
¾ cup raspberry jam or jelly

1

Use plenty of butter to grease the base and sides of a 10 x 15-inch jelly roll pan or rimmed baking sheet, then line the base with parchment paper. Preheat the oven to 400°F. Put the milk and butter in a small pan and heat gently until the butter melts. Set aside (it will need to be warm when you use it).

2

Put the eggs and the sugar in a large bowl and whisk with an electric mixer at medium speed until thick, moussey, and doubled in volume—about 5 minutes.

3

Stir the cornstarch, flour, and salt together, then sift them on top of the eggs. Fold together well using a large metal spoon or spatula, cutting and lifting the flour through the foam instead of stirring it. This will preserve the air bubbles and ensure a light and fluffy cake.

4

Pour the warm butter and milk around the edge of the batter bowl. Using the large spoon or spatula, fold until evenly combined. The liquid can pool at the bottom of the bowl, so be persistent, trying not to knock out too much air.

5

Carefully pour the batter into the prepared pan, then tilt it slowly from side to side, letting the batter run into the corners. If it still looks uneven, spread out the batter very gently with a spatula. Don't worry if you see a little dry flour or ribbons of butter—just work them in gently. The batter will completely fill the pan, but don't worry, it won't spill over as it bakes.

6

Bake for 10 minutes, or until it is golden, has risen, and the edges have shrunk away from the sides of the pan. Meanwhile, dust a larger sheet of parchment paper with 2 tablespoons sugar. Loosen the edges of the cake with an icing spatula, then sprinkle the remaining sugar on top.

7

Swiftly flip the cake onto the sugared parchment paper. Carefully peel off the paper that lined the pan. Using a serrated knife, trim about ½ inch off from each edge. Score a line into the cake about 1 inch in from the short end nearest you. This will make it easier to roll.

8

While the cake is still hot, roll it up from the short end, rolling the sugared paper inside the cake. Don't rush things, and if a few cracks appear, don't worry.

9

Cover the cake in a clean dish towel and let cool until just warm.

10

Unwrap and unroll the cake, then spread it with the jam. Roll the cake up again, using one hand to guide it and the other to pull the sugared paper underneath it upwards. This will help keep the spiral fairly tight.

FILLING WITH CREAM?
To fill with whipped cream (see page 48) or buttercream frosting (see page 46), the cake must be cold. Whipped cream can go straight on top of the jam. For buttercream, spread it out first, then cover it with jam.

11

Place on a serving plate, seam-side down. It's best eaten on the day it is made.

Iced Gingerbread Cookies

Preparation time: 20 minutes,
plus firming and cooling
Baking time: 9–11 minutes per batch
Makes about 14 gingerbread men,
or 24 smaller shapes

These happy little cookies are perfect
for an afternoon of baking with
children, as the dough can handle
plenty of squishing and rolling without
becoming tough. The level of spice
should please adult tastebuds too.
For a darker color and bittersweet
flavor, replace the syrup with black
treacle or molasses.

For the cookies

1 stick (½ cup) butter, plus extra
   for greasing
1 packed cup dark brown sugar
⅓ cup golden syrup, such as Lyle's,
   or corn syrup
1 egg
2¾ cups all-purpose flour,
   plus extra for rolling
1 tsp baking soda
1 tbsp ground ginger
2 tsp ground cinnamon
¼ tsp salt

To decorate

1⅔ cups confectioners' sugar
1 egg white or 2 tbsp lemon juice
   (see Tip)
sparkles or dragees (optional)

1
Put the butter, sugar, and syrup in a large pan, then gently heat until the butter has melted. Beat the egg.

2
Let cool for 5 minutes, then beat the egg into the pan. Mix the flour, baking soda, spices, and salt, then sift into the saucepan. Stir together to make a shiny dough.

3
Turn out the dough onto the work surface, split it in half, then knead briefly to make 2 smooth balls. Squash into flat disks, wrap well in plastic wrap, then chill in the fridge until firm (this will take about 2 hours, or you can leave it overnight).

4
When ready to bake, grease 2 baking sheets with a little butter, then line with parchment paper. Preheat the oven to 350°F. Lightly flour the work surface and use a rolling pin to roll the dough to ⅛ inch thick. Cut out shapes and carefully lift them onto the lined sheets, giving each cookie plenty of space. Squash together, re-roll, and cut out the trimmings. You'll find the cookies come out of the cutter cleanly if you dip the cutter in a little flour first.

5

For softer cookies, bake for 9 minutes, or until golden all over (they will rise a little in the oven, then flatten out), or for cookies with snap, bake for 11 minutes. Let cool for 5 minutes on the baking sheet, then transfer to a rack to cool completely. Re-use the sheets for the rest of the dough.

TREE DECORATIONS
To make your cookies into Christmas tree decorations, punch a hole in the cooked dough (while still hot) using a plastic drinking straw or small pastry bag tip, or something like a pointy chopstick. Take care when handling the hot dough. Thread with ribbon to hang from the tree.

6

To make the icing, separate the egg (see page 127) and put the white in a clean bowl. Sift the confectioners' sugar on top, stir it in slowly at first to incorporate, then beat well until smooth. To decorate, either drizzle teaspoons of the icing over your cookies, or spoon it into a disposable pastry bag or food storage bag, snip off the very end and use it to pipe patterns. Decorate with sparkles or dragees, if you like.

ROYAL ICING
Icing made with egg white is known as royal icing. It has a bright whiteness to it, and sets very firmly. You can use store-bought pasteurized egg whites if you are concerned about using raw eggs, or replace the egg white with lemon juice instead. Start with 2 tablespoons, then add more if needed.

7

Let the icing set for about 1 hour or until firm and dry, before eating, hanging on the tree, or packing into an airtight container.

Vanilla Sponge Cake

Preparation time: 30 minutes,
plus cooling
Baking time: 25 minutes
Makes 12 slices

This simple yet special butter cake, stacked with buttercream and jam, is a classic family bake and a regular in my house. The layers are tall and delicate, but keep very well for three days, and freeze well too. It's also good with the chocolate frosting on page 134.

For the cake

2 sticks (1 cup) soft butter,
   plus extra for greasing
1½ cups sugar, preferably superfine
5 eggs, room temperature
2¼ cups all-purpose flour
2 tbsp cornstarch
1 tbsp baking powder
¼ tsp salt
½ cup milk, at room temperature
1 tsp vanilla paste or extract
2 tbsp vegetable oil

For the buttercream frosting

7 tbsp soft butter
1¼ cups confectioners' sugar,
   plus extra for dusting
1 tsp vanilla extract or paste
1 tsp milk (if needed)
½ cup strawberry jam

1
Preheat the oven to 350°F. Use a little butter to grease two 8-inch round cake pans with removable bottoms, then line the bottoms with parchment paper. Put the butter and sugar in a large bowl, then beat with an electric mixer until creamy and very pale.

2
Crack the eggs into a measuring cup. Pour 1 egg into the bowl with the butter and sugar, then beat it into the creamed butter and sugar mixture until it looks fluffy and light. Add the next egg and repeat. If the batter starts to look a little slimy at any point, beat in 1 tablespoon of the flour.

3
Stir the flour, cornstarch, baking powder, and salt together in a bowl. Put the milk, vanilla, and oil in the eggy cup (to save washing another dish). Sift half of the flour on top of the batter, then fold in the milk mixture using a spatula or large metal spoon. Finish with the rest of the flour mixture and keep folding until you have a thick, smooth batter. A big blob of batter should drop (but not slide) away from the spatula if you give it a little shake. If it seems to stick on, then the batter may be a little dry; add 1 tablespoon more milk.

SHORTCUT?
If you want to make this cake more quickly, cream the butter and sugar together as in step 1, then add the rest of the ingredients, plus an extra 1 teaspoon baking powder, and beat them in with the electric mixer, taking care not to overwork the batter once it looks smooth and creamy. Cakes made this way can have a slightly less delicate texture and a lower rise, but if you're in a hurry, then go for it.

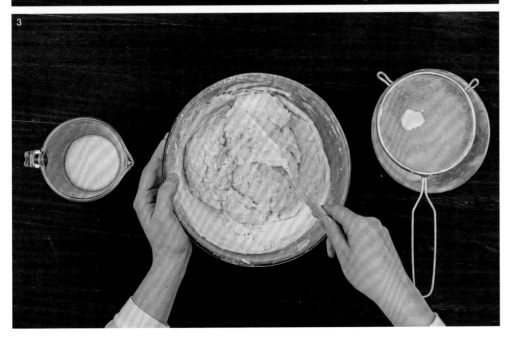

4

Scrape the batter into the prepared pans and smooth the tops. For a nice, even cake, try to ensure each one has more or less the same amount in it.

5

Bake for 25 minutes, or until the cakes are golden, have risen, spring back to the touch, and a skewer inserted into the center comes away clean. If the cakes are browning unevenly, they can be safely turned around after about 15 minutes, or once they have risen evenly and the surface looks dry. Be quick while you do this, to preserve heat in the oven. Let cool in the pans for 10 minutes, then turn out. I like to peel the paper from the bottom, put this on the cooling rack crumb-side down, then put the cakes on top.

6

Make the buttercream frosting. Beat the butter until very soft. Sift in the confectioners' sugar, add the vanilla, then gradually work the sugar in before increasing the beater speed and beating until smooth, pale, and creamy. If it seems stiff, add 1 teaspoon milk.

7

Put one of the sponges on a serving plate, then spread with the buttercream. Top with the jam.

8

Sandwich with the second sponge, then sift a little more confectioners' sugar over the top.

TRY IT WITH WHIPPED CREAM
Whip 1 cup heavy cream with 1 teaspoon vanilla and 1–2 tablespoons confectioners' sugar (to your taste), until thickened but not stiff. Spread the jam first, then top with the cream.

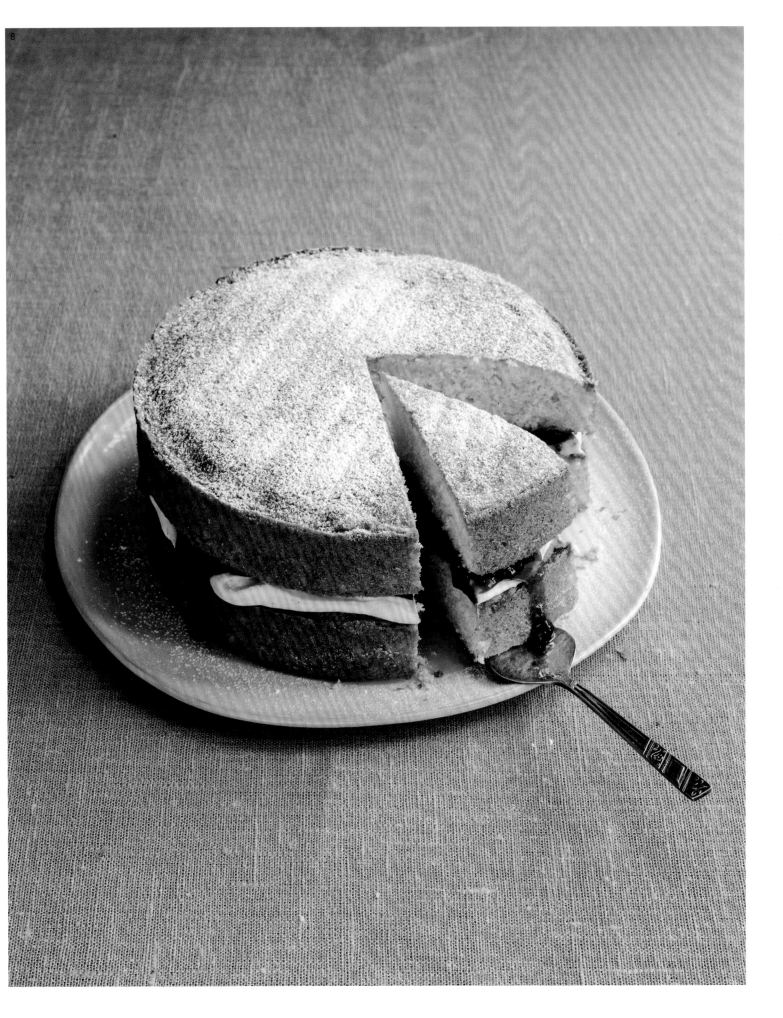

Chocolate & Nut Banana Bread

Preparation time: 10 minutes
Baking time: about 1 hour 10 minutes
Cuts into 10 slices

There's no excuse not to use up those spotty brown bananas hanging around in the kitchen when the method for making banana bread is as straightforward as this. Mash, fold and bake, and you're well on your way to breakfast or snack-time happiness.

---

1 stick (½ cup) butter
3 medium over-ripe bananas
   (to yield 1–1¼ cups mashed fruit)
2 eggs
⅓ cup maple syrup
⅓ cup plus 1 tbsp sugar
2 cups all-purpose flour
¼ tsp salt
2 tsp baking powder
¾ cup walnut pieces
⅓ cup bittersweet chocolate chips
   (or chopped bittersweet
   chocolate)

1
Preheat the oven to 325°F. Grease an 8½ x 4½-inch loaf pan with a little of the butter, then line the base and two narrow ends of the pan with one long strip of parchment paper. Melt the butter in a saucepan. Using a fork, mash the bananas in a large bowl, until they're as smooth as possible.

2
Pour the melted butter into the bananas, then add the eggs and maple syrup. Beat everything together with the fork until the eggs are really well broken up. Mix the sugar, flour, salt, and baking powder in a bowl, then sift onto the banana mixture. Using a spatula, fold in the flour mixture to make a smooth cake batter. Fold in most of the nuts and chocolate chips, saving a few to sprinkle on the top. Pour the batter into the pan, then sprinkle the reserved nuts and chocolate across the top.

3
Bake for 1 hour 10 minutes, or until it is golden, has risen well, and a skewer inserted into the middle of the bread comes out clean, or with a few damp crumbs attached. The time can vary depending on how ripe your bananas are, as riper bananas will make a looser batter. Let cool in the pan for 15 minutes or so, then lift it out onto a cooling rack. Serve thickly sliced, with a pat of butter if you like.

IT'S A KEEPER
The cake will keep in an airtight container for up to 5 days, and can be frozen. To revive less-than-perfect banana bread, toast it lightly, or warm gently in the oven or microwave.

Lemon & Raisin Pancakes

Preparation time: 5 minutes
Cooking time: 15 minutes
Makes about 16 with the raisins,
12 without

Griddle cakes, drop scones, silver
dollars, Scotch pancakes—whatever
you call them, these fluffy treats are
great for any time of day: breakfast,
brunch, or when the kids are home
from school and hungry. I like
mine with lemon and raisins, but the
plain batter is great cooked up with
blueberries too, or stacked high
with crisp bacon and maple syrup.

1⅓ cups plus 1 tbsp
    all-purpose flour
1½ tsp baking powder
½ tsp baking soda
2 tbsp sugar
¼ tsp salt
1 lemon
1 cup buttermilk (or see Tip)
2 tbsp milk
1 tsp vanilla extract
1 egg
½ cup raisins or golden raisins
    (optional)
about 2 tbsp vegetable oil
butter and maple syrup, to serve

1
If you're planning to serve the pancakes all at once, rather than in batches straight from the pan, preheat the oven to 275°F, and put a plate in to warm. Put the flour, baking powder, and baking soda in a large bowl. Add the sugar and salt, then whisk together to combine. Finely grate in the zest of the lemon.

WHY WHISK?
I often use a whisk instead of a sieve when all the dry ingredients are a similar texture (it wouldn't work with lumpier soft brown sugar in the bowl, for example). The whisk mixes and aerates—and there's a bit less to clean at the end of cooking.

2
Make a well in the center of the flour, then add the buttermilk, milk, and vanilla, and crack in the egg.

CAN'T FIND BUTTERMILK?
Mix 1 cup milk with 2 tablespoons lemon juice and let stand for 5 minutes. Use it in place of the buttermilk. You won't need the extra 2 tablespoons milk.

3
Using the whisk, start to mix the flour into the egg and buttermilk; keep going until everything is incorporated, then beat well to make a thick, smooth batter. Stir in the raisins, if using.

4

Put a large nonstick frying pan or flat griddle over medium heat and add 1 teaspoon of the vegetable oil. Let it heat for a few seconds, swirl it to coat the pan, then add tablespoons of the batter to the pan, spaced well apart. The mixture should sizzle as soon as it hits the pan, and spread out a little. Nudge it around with the spoon to make neatish circles. Cook for 1 minute on the first side, or until bubbles start to appear and a few of them pop on the surface of the pancakes. Keep the heat steady.

5

Using a spatula, flip the pancakes over to reveal golden bottoms (starting with the one you first poured, so that they all have the same cooking time), and cook for another 30 seconds–1 minute, or until they have puffed in the middle and feel springy when pressed. Remove from the pan, transfer to a plate, and keep warm in the oven while you cook the rest.

GETTING AHEAD
Buttermilk pancakes are easy to reheat. Give them a few seconds in the microwave, toast under the broiler or in a toaster oven, or wrap in foil and reheat in the oven at 350°F for 10 minutes. I like them cold, too.

6

Serve the warm pancakes with a pat of softened butter, a drizzle of maple syrup, and a squeeze from the lemon, if you like.

Rocky Road

Preparation time: 10 minutes,
plus setting time
Makes 16 squares

OK, this isn't strictly speaking
baking, but I couldn't leave out such
an all-round people-pleaser of a
recipe. I like to use ginger cookies in
my rocky road, which gives a spicy
edge, but really any crunchy cookie
will do, such as graham crackers,
Rich Tea, or even Oreos for a double
chocolate hit.

½ stick (¼ cup) butter, plus extra
    for greasing
14 oz bittersweet chocolate,
    60% cocoa solids
2 tbsp golden syrup, such as Lyle's,
    or corn syrup
a pinch of salt
1 cup mixed nuts
6 oz crunchy cookies
3½ oz marshmallows
½ cup plump raisins,
    or other dried fruit
1 tbsp confectioners' sugar

1

Use a little butter to grease a 9-inch square baking pan, then line it with parchment paper. To melt the chocolate, first half-fill a medium pan with water and bring it to a simmer. Break the chocolate into squares and cut the butter into pieces, then put them in a large heatproof bowl. Sit the bowl over the pan of water, making sure that the bowl doesn't touch the water. (This is sometimes called a bain marie or double boiler.)

CHOOSING CHOCOLATE
If you're unable to find 60% cocoa content chocolate, a mix of half 70% cocoa and half 50% cocoa chocolate is every bit as good.

2

With the pan over very low heat, let the chocolate and butter melt together, stirring now and again, until smooth and silky. Now stir in the syrup and salt and take the bowl off the heat.

3

While you wait for the chocolate to melt, roughly chop any larger nuts (such as brazils, if there are some in your mix). Crush or break the cookies into smaller chunks. Snip the marshmallows in half.

4

Scoop about ½ cup of the chocolate from the bowl and set aside. Toss all of the cookie chunks, nuts, marshmallows, and raisins, or whatever you are using, into the rest of the chocolate and stir well with a spatula until everything is well coated.

5

Spread the rocky road mixture into the pan, then add the "asphalt": that is, spoon the reserved chocolate over the mixture to cover. It won't be perfectly smooth, but that's all part of the charm.

6

Let the rocky road chill in the fridge for about 3 hours, or longer if you like, until very firm. Remove from the pan, peel off the paper from the edges, cut into squares, and dust with the confectioners' sugar.

7

Store in the fridge or a cool place for up to 3 days.

TURKISH ROAD
Swap half the marshmallows for pieces of Turkish delight.

ROMAN ROAD
For an Italian panforte-inspired twist, replace half the raisins with finely chopped crystallized orange peel. Use amaretti cookies and add 1 teaspoon ground cinnamon and ½ teaspoon ground nutmeg, plus a pinch of ground cloves, if you like.

Vanilla Fruit Scones

Preparation time: 15 minutes
Baking time: 12 minutes
Makes 10

A perfectly fluffy scone is a simple pleasure: quick and thrifty to make, but so delicious, especially when served just warm with cream or butter and a good dollop of jam or lemon curd. The most important thing to remember is not to knead the dough, which will quickly make your scones heavy.

3¼ cups all-purpose flour, plus
    extra for dusting
2 tsp baking powder
¼ tsp baking soda
¼ tsp salt
½ stick plus 3 tbsp (¼ cup plus
    3 tbsp) cold butter
¼ cup plus 1 tbsp sugar
½ cup golden raisins or your choice
    of dried fruit (optional)
1 cup less 1 tbsp milk
2 tsp lemon juice
1 tsp vanilla extract
1 egg

1
Preheat the oven to 425°F. Put a large baking sheet in the oven to heat up. Mix the flour, baking powder, baking soda, and salt, then sift into a large bowl. Cut the butter into cubes and add it to the bowl.

2
Rub the cold butter into the flour using your fingertips, until it looks like breadcrumbs. If you have a food processor, simply process the butter into the dry ingredients instead, then pour into a large bowl.

COLD BUTTER
Fluffy, flaky scones need to be made with really cold butter. If it's a hot day and the butter begins to feel greasy as you rub it in, pop the bowl in the fridge for 10 minutes before continuing.

3
Stir in the sugar, and the dried fruit if you're using it. I've made this a separate step because I've forgotten to add the sugar so many times when making scones, and I'm determined that you won't do the same!

4
Heat the milk in a small pan (or in the microwave for a few seconds) until warm, then add the lemon juice and vanilla. Let sit for a few minutes until it turns a little bit lumpy. Beat the egg, then add 2 tablespoons of it to the lumpy milk mixture. Set the rest of the egg aside.

MILK OR BUTTERMILK?
Souring the milk lightens the dough by activating the baking soda and boosting the rise. You can add ¾ cup of buttermilk or yogurt instead, and loosen with ¼ cup milk. Omit the lemon juice, but don't forget to add the egg.

5

Pour the soured milk evenly over the dry ingredients, working it into the flour with a table knife. Keep mixing until all the liquid is incorporated and you have a soft, rough dough. Don't worry if you miss a few crumbs at the bottom of the bowl; it's best not to overmix it.

6

Flour your hands and the work surface thoroughly. Turn the dough out onto it and sprinkle a little flour on top. Fold the dough over itself a couple of times just to smooth it a little (it's essential not to overwork it at this point), then pat it into a 1¼-inch thick round. Try to make sure the smoothest part of the dough ends up being the top.

7

Using a 2½-inch round cookie cutter, cut out 6 scones. Dip the cutter into some flour between each cut to stop it sticking. Don't twist the cutter in the dough—the aim is to have a good, clean cut. Carefully press the remaining dough together and cut out the rest; remember not to overwork it.

8

Brush the tops of the scones with some of the remaining egg.

9

Remove the hot baking sheet from the oven and sprinkle it with flour. Carefully place the scones on it, spacing them out evenly. The heat will give the scones a head start.

10

Bake for 12 minutes, or until golden and well risen, and sound hollow when tapped underneath. You may need to turn the pan around after 8 minutes to ensure an even color. Cool on a wire rack. For scones with a softer crust, wrap in a clean, dry dish towel before cooling.

Malted Milk Chocolate Birthday Cake

Preparation time: 30 minutes,
plus cooling
Baking time: 30 minutes
Makes 16 generous or 32
small pieces

There can be a lot of pressure
to provide a homemade birthday
cake that everyone will enjoy. This
no-stress sheet cake keeps well
if you want to get ahead, and is
deliciously chocolatey but not too
rich. It's easily cut into squares once
the candles have been blown out.

For the cake
1¼ sticks (½ cup plus 2 tbsp)
    soft butter
2¾ cups all-purpose flour
¼ cup good-quality cocoa powder
2 tbsp malted milk powder,
    such as Horlicks
1 tsp baking soda
2 tsp baking powder
¼ tsp salt
1½ packed cups light brown sugar
1¼ cups milk
½ cup plus 2 tbsp vegetable oil
1 tsp vanilla extract

For the frosting
7 oz semi-sweet chocolate,
    about 50% cocoa solids
½ cup milk
¼ cup cocoa powder
2 tbsp malted milk powder
1¼ sticks (½ cup plus 2 tbsp)
    soft butter
2¼ cups confectioners' sugar
a handful of colored candy-coated
    chocolates, and candles

1
Preheat the oven to 350°F. Make the cake batter first. Put the butter in a saucepan and melt it gently. Using a pastry brush, use a little of the butter to grease a 9 x 13-inch sheet cake pan. Line the pan with parchment paper.

2
Mix the flour, cocoa, malted milk powder, baking soda, baking powder, and salt, then sift into a large bowl. Add the sugar and break up any lumps with your fingers. Make a well in the center of the dry ingredients, pushing most of it to the sides of the bowl. Whisk the milk, oil, and vanilla into the melted butter and pour them into the well.

3
Using a whisk, mix the flour mixture into the well, slowly at first. Once mixed, give it a good beat until smooth and evenly blended. Pour into the prepared pan.

4
Bake for 30 minutes, until the cake has risen, is firm, and slightly shrunken from the sides. A skewer inserted into the center should come out clean. Leave in the pan for 10 minutes, then turn out onto a cooling rack and cool completely.

5
For the frosting, break the chocolate into a heatproof bowl and place it over a pan of barely simmering water, making sure the bowl doesn't touch the water. Let the chocolate melt for about 5 minutes, stirring once or twice, until smooth. Alternatively, microwave in 20-second bursts, stirring each time. Let cool a little.

NO EGGS?
This cake is egg-free, in case you wondered.

6

Heat the milk in a small pan or the microwave until steaming hot. Sift the cocoa and malted milk powder into a large bowl, then slowly stir in the hot milk to make a smooth paste. Let cool for a few minutes.

7

Now add the butter to the paste, sift in the confectioners' sugar, and beat together with an electric mixer until very creamy. Follow with the melted, cooled chocolate, to make a silky, soft frosting.

8

Transfer the cooled cake to a board or large, flat plate, then spread the frosting all over it. It will firm a little as it cools, so try to create your swoops and swirls fairly quickly.

9

Sprinkle the cake with the candies and top with colored candles. Let the frosting set for a little while if you can, although it's delicious—if a little more messy—eaten immediately too. The cake can be made up to 2 days ahead and kept in a cool place, well wrapped, or, if frosted, loosely covered on its board.

PATRIOTIC CAKE
For all the patriots out there, how about arranging the decorations in the colors of your national flag?

HALLOWEEN CAKE
Choose candy insects and other gruesome things to top the cake, or stand long, thin cookies up in the frosting, to look like gravestones.

EASTER CAKE
Scatter the frosting with pastel-colored chocolate eggs.

Classic Crusty Bread

Preparation time: 20 minutes,
plus rising and proofing time
Baking time: 25–30 minutes
Makes 1 large loaf

Baking a loaf of bread from scratch
has to be one of the most satisfying
tasks ever. There's little to prevent
novice or rusty bakers from turning
out a loaf to be proud of, no matter
how much time you have to spare.
Most people are hooked after one
loaf, which is why I've included
a few easy variations to turn your
hand to next (see page 72).

4 cups bread flour, plus extra
   for dusting
2 tsp instant dry yeast
1 tsp sugar
2 tsp salt
about 1¼ cups warm water
2 tbsp olive oil, plus extra
   for greasing

1

Put all the dry ingredients in a large bowl. Mix the water with the oil. The water should be pleasantly warm, but nowhere near hot; excess heat can kill the yeast.

2

Mix the dry ingredients together and, while stirring, pour in the water and oil. Keep working everything together until most of the dry flour has disappeared. The dough will be rough and a little sticky.

GETTING THE RIGHT TEXTURE

If a dough doesn't form, add a splash more water. A wetter dough will produce a tastier loaf in the end, and flours can differ a lot in moisture content, depending on their age, the weather, and where the wheat was grown.

3

Dust the work surface with flour, then turn the dough out onto it. Flour the top of the dough and your hands, then begin to knead. Avoid adding too much flour as you knead. If the dough really sticks to the surface a lot, scrape away any bits with a knife, wash and dry your hands and start again, dusting the surface, the dough and your hands with a little more flour.

HOW TO KNEAD

As long as the dough is stretched and folded enough to make it springy and smooth, it doesn't really matter what your kneading technique is. I push the dough down with my left hand, grip it with my right and push it away. Then fold the dough back over itself, rotate it a quarter turn, and repeat. If you have a stand mixer with a dough hook (or some food processors have dough "blades"), that's a good—but less therapeutic—time saver.

4

Keep going until the dough feels very springy or elastic and silky smooth. To test if it's ready, gather it into a ball, tucking all the edges into the middle. Turn the ball over to reveal the smooth side. Keeping the dough pinched into a ball shape with one hand, press into it with the other hand. If the indent made by your finger stays there, it's not ready. If it springs out again, you're ready to move on.

5

Now let the dough rise. Grease a large bowl with 1 tablespoon oil, add the dough, then turn it around in the oil a few times to coat. Cover with plastic wrap. You can also use a dish towel to cover the bowl, or grease a large food storage bag, pop the dough into it and seal it, leaving plenty of room for rising.

6
Leave the dough in a warm (but not hot) place for about an hour, or until doubled in size.

OVERNIGHT RISING
I often make the bread dough the night before, then leave it in the fridge overnight instead of in a warm place. Letting it rise more slowly means that the bread has a more complex flavor; let it come up to room temperature the next day, then continue.

7
Turn out the pillowy dough onto a floured surface, then press it out into a rectangle that's about 8 x 11 inches, the size of a standard piece of paper. Do not knead it, or it will become stretchy again, and difficult to shape. Fold the bottom of the rectangle up, and the bottom half down, to make a sort of sausage. Pinch the edges together firmly.

8

Dust a baking sheet with flour, then lift the dough onto it, smooth side up. Pat it back into shape if needed. Loosely cover with oiled plastic wrap or the dish towel, then let rise again (it's known as proofing at this stage) for 30 minutes, or until almost doubled in size. Poke the side of the dough; it doesn't spring back, it's ready to bake. Preheat the oven to 425°F.

9

Sprinkle the top of the bread with more flour, then slash the top with a sharp knife. This is important, as it gives the bread somewhere to "grow" in the oven.

10

Bake for 25–30 minutes, or until well risen, golden, and crisp. When you think it's ready, double check by carefully turning the bread over. Tap the base; it should sound hollow. If not, return to the oven and check in 10 minutes. Let cool, open to the air for a crusty crust, or wrapped in a clean dish towel for a soft crust.

WHOLE-WHEAT SEEDED BREAD
Swap half the flour for whole-wheat bread flour plus 3 tablespoons mixed seeds. You may need to add a little more liquid; try milk instead of water. Sprinkle with more seeds before slashing and baking.

ROSEMARY FOCACCIA
Press the risen dough into a 9 x 13-inch pan and proof. Just before baking, poke holes all over the dough, scatter with fresh rosemary sprigs and flaky sea salt, then drizzle with extra-virgin olive oil. Bake until risen and golden.

PIZZA CRUSTS
Cut the risen dough into 4 pieces, roll out thinly on large baking sheets, add the toppings, then bake immediately at 475°F until crisp.

MORNING COFFEE
&
AFTERNOON TEA

Classic Shortbread

Preparation time: 15 minutes,
plus chilling and cooling
Baking time: 1 hour 10 minutes
Makes 12 pieces

Homemade shortbread takes
some beating. The quality of the
ingredients will make a difference in
the final flavor, so here's one recipe
for which I would invest in a slightly
more expensive brand of unsalted
butter. For shortbread with extra
crunch, substitute ½ cup of the flour
with the same quantity of rice flour.

2 sticks (1 cup) soft butter
½ cup sugar, ideally superfine,
   plus extra for sprinkling
¼ tsp salt
1 tsp vanilla extract
2¼ cups all-purpose flour

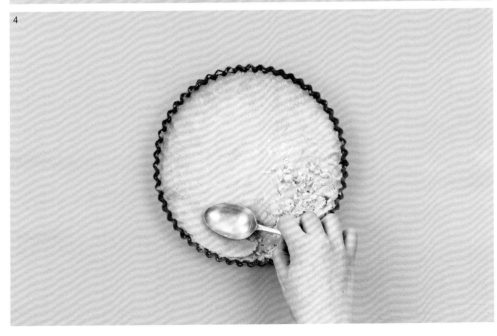

1

Prepare a 9-inch round fluted tart pan with a removable bottom by greasing right into the ribs of the pan with a little of the butter. Put the rest of the butter in a large bowl and beat well with a wooden spoon or an electric mixer until creamy and very pale.

2

Add the sugar, salt, and vanilla and beat again until even creamier and paler.

3

Sift the flour into the bowl. Using a spatula, gently fold and cut the flour into the mixture to make an evenly blended dough. Don't overdo it: the more you mix, the tougher your shortbread will be, so be careful here.

4

Press the dough into the pan, then smooth it with the back of a spoon. If you find the spoon is dragging a little on the surface, sprinkle a little flour over the top and have another try. Any rough bits at the very edges of the pan can be pressed flat with your fingertips.

DIFFERENT PANS?
If you'd like to make this in a regular 9-inch round cake pan, that's fine, or you can press it into an 8-inch square pan instead, and cut the shortbread into rectangles. A pan with a removable bottom makes it easier to take the cooked shortbread out, but it isn't essential. The cooking time will be the same.

For a quicker version, roll the dough into a sausage about 2½ inches across, wrap in plastic wrap and chill in the freezer until firm. Slice into ½-inch rounds, then bake on a parchment-lined baking sheet at 350°F for 20–25 minutes, or until golden.

5

Mark the edge of the shortbread with the tines of a fork, then cut the dough into 12 wedges. I do this in quarters first, then cut each quarter into three, to get nicely even pieces. Prick 2 holes in each piece of shortbread, going right to the base of the pan. Chill the shortbread for 20 minutes (or longer if you like), until very firm. Preheat the oven to 325°F while the shortbread chills.

6

Bake for 1 hour 10 minutes, or until golden and sandy all across the top. If you've used rice flour it might take a little less time, so check after 1 hour. Let cool in the pan for 5 minutes, then re-mark the wedges and fork holes, if you like. Sprinkle with 1–2 teaspoons sugar and let cool in the pan, on a rack.

7

Cut the shortbread into triangles to serve, then store in an airtight container for up to 1 week.

ORANGE SHORTBREAD
Add the finely grated zest of an orange to the mixture at step 2.

LAVENDER SHORTBREAD
Add 1 tablespoon chopped, unsprayed lavender flowers to the sugar and let it infuse for a few minutes before use. Rosemary works well too.

PECAN SHORTBREAD
Add ½ cup chopped pecans to the dough. I like to add an extra pinch of salt to this one.

CHOCOLATE SHORTBREAD
Melt 2 oz bittersweet chocolate (70% cocoa solids). Separate the cooled cookies on a rack, then drizzle with the chocolate instead of sprinkling with the extra sugar.

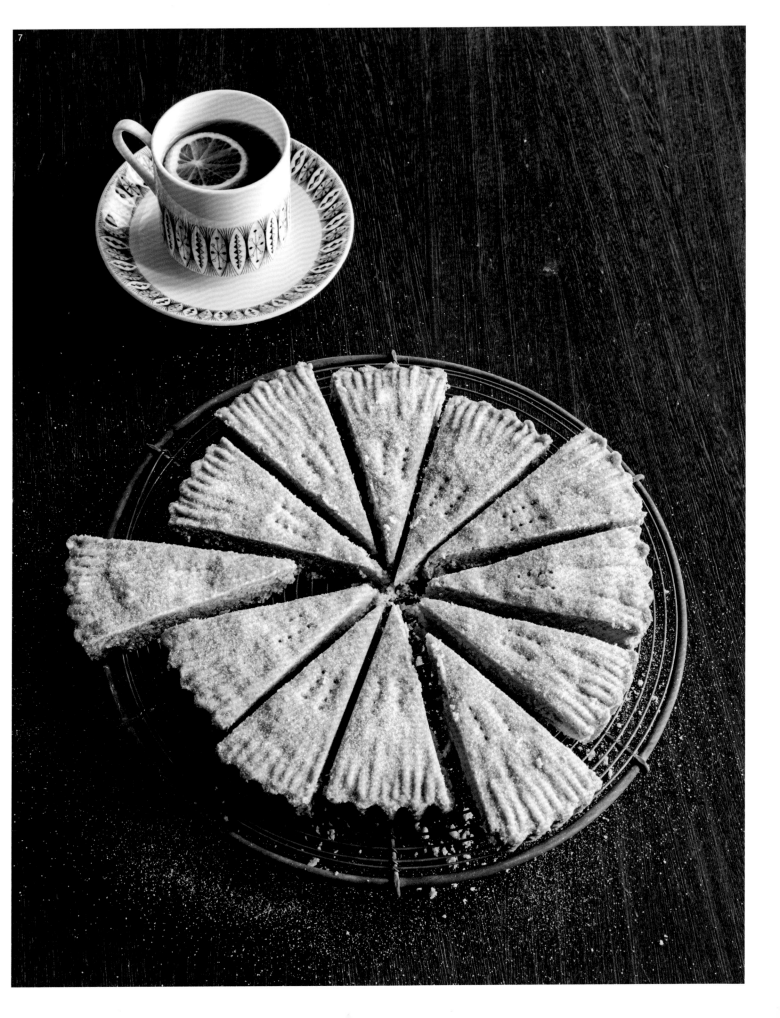

Zucchini-Lemon Cupcakes with Mascarpone Frosting

Preparation time: 20 minutes,
plus cooling
Baking time: 20 minutes
Makes 12 cupcakes

Zucchini, like carrot in carrot cakes, adds a soft freshness to these cupcakes rather than any particular flavor, and is well worth a try. A quick lemon drizzle ramps up the zesty flavor in these little cakes, and a luscious lemon curd mascarpone finishes them off beautifully.

For the cupcakes

7 oz zucchini (about 1–2; smaller
   ones are better)
1½ sticks (¾ cup) soft butter,
   plus extra for greasing
1 lemon
¾ cup sugar, plus 1 tbsp extra
1⅔ cups all-purpose flour
   (or see Tip)
2½ tsp baking powder
¼ tsp salt
3 eggs, room temperature
1 tbsp poppy seeds

For the frosting

½ cup good-quality lemon curd
1 cup mascarpone
2 tsp poppy seeds

1

Coarsely grate the zucchini, skins and all. You should have about 1½ cups. Spread them out between paper towels or on a clean dish towel and set aside for a few minutes while you get everything else ready.

2

Preheat the oven to 350°F. Grease the holes of a 12-cup nonstick muffin pan, or use 12 deep paper liners in an ungreased pan if you prefer. Finely grate the zest from the lemon and squeeze the juice. Put the zest, 2 tablespoons juice, and the butter and sugar in a large mixing bowl. Beat using an electric mixer or wooden spoon until creamy and pale.

3

Mix the flour, baking powder, and salt together, then sift on top of the butter and sugar mixture. Crack in the eggs, then beat everything together until evenly blended. Try not to overwork the batter once the flour has gone in.

TRY A DIFFERENT FLOUR
These cupcakes are also delicious made with spelt flour, or a 50:50 mix of spelt and all-purpose, or whole-wheat and all-purpose. Both give a slightly nuttier taste and texture to the end result. Whole-wheat flour can absorb more liquid than regular flour, so add 1 tablespoon milk if the batter seems thick.

4

Fold in the poppy seeds and grated zucchini, then spoon into the prepared pan. The cups will seem fairly full, which is fine.

5

Bake for 20 minutes, or until they have risen and are golden, and a skewer inserted into one of the center cakes comes out clean. Mix the rest of the lemon juice with the extra sugar and let it melt together, stirring occasionally, while the cakes cook. Poke holes in the tops of the cakes with a toothpick and spoon the syrup over them. Let cool for 10 minutes, then remove to a cooling rack.

6

To make the frosting, put the lemon curd and mascarpone in a large bowl and beat with a wooden spoon or spatula until smooth and evenly blended. Dollop it onto the cooled cakes just before eating and swirl with a spoon or small icing spatula.

7

Sprinkle with the poppy seeds to finish. The cupcakes are best enjoyed fresh, but keep any leftover cakes in a cool place or the fridge once the frosting has been added.

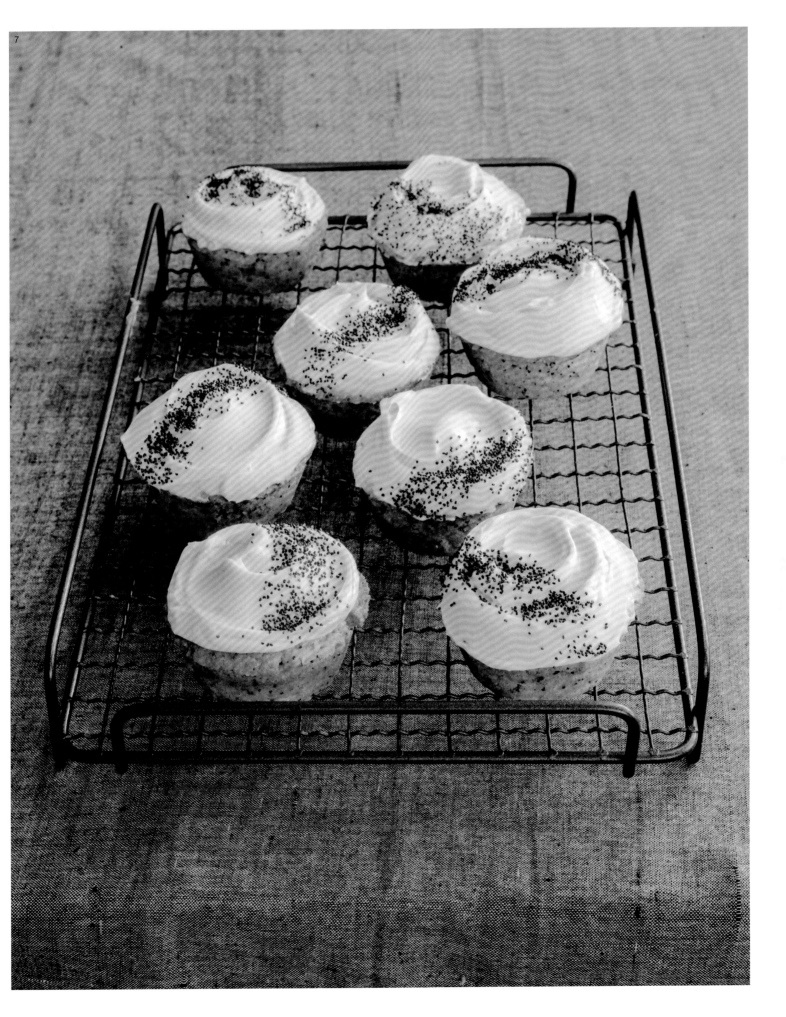

Jaffa Marble Loaf

Preparation time: 30 minutes
Baking time: 55–60 minutes
Makes 8–10 slices

With its hidden swirls of chocolate and zesty orange, this is a fun cake to make—and to cut in front of a hungry audience. The dark chocolate topping keeps the balance in favor of bitter rather than sweet; for young children you may want to use milk chocolate instead.

For the cake

1½ sticks (¾ cup) soft butter,
   plus extra for greasing
1 large orange
¾ cup plus 2 tbsp sugar
1⅓ cups all-purpose flour
¼ tsp salt
1 tsp baking powder
3 eggs, room temperature
3 tbsp vegetable oil
2 tbsp cocoa powder

For the topping

4 oz bittersweet chocolate,
   70% cocoa solids
2 tbsp golden syrup, such as Lyle's,
   or corn syrup

1

Grease an 8½ x 4½-inch loaf pan, with butter, then line it with 2 strips of parchment paper that hang over the sides. Preheat the oven to 325°F. Finely grate the zest from the orange, then squeeze the juice.

2

Put the butter, sugar, and most of the orange zest in a large bowl. Using an electric mixer, beat together until pale and creamy.

3

Mix the flour, salt, and baking powder, then sift on top of the creamed mixture. Add the eggs and oil.

4

Beat everything together until smooth, adding 3 tablespoons of the orange juice to bring the batter to soft dropping consistency.

SOFT DROPPING CONSISTENCY
A spoonful of cake batter should drop easily into the bowl when given a gentle shake. If it resists, it's a sign that the batter is too stiff and will make a dry cake. To get a moist, tender cake, recipes often call for a liquid, in this case the orange juice, to be added after the flour has gone in. The amount of liquid you need will depend on the recipe and the type and age of the flour you are using. The oil in this recipe also helps to keep it moist, so it's ideal for making ahead for a bake sale, or the kitchen cupboard.

5

Spoon half the cake batter into another bowl, then sift in the cocoa powder and mix until evenly blended. If it seems dry compared to the white batter, add another tablespoon of orange juice.

6

Spoon the chocolate and orange cake batters into the pan in alternating spoonfuls until both bowls are empty. Stir a skewer or chopstick through the batter a couple of times to ripple the blobs together and encourage swirls in the middle of the cake.

7

Bake for 55–60 minutes, or until it is golden and has risen all the way to the middle. Insert a skewer into the center of the cake; if it comes out clean, it is ready. Cool in the pan for 10 minutes, then lift out using the lining paper and cool on a wire rack. For the topping, melt the chocolate either in a heatproof bowl over a pan of water, or in the microwave (see page 119). Stir in the syrup and reserved orange zest.

8

Spread the topping over the cooled cake, then let it set for an hour or so, until firm.

9

Slice the cake thickly and serve, or wrap and keep in an airtight container for up to 3 days.

MOCHA-CHOCOLATE
MARBLE LOAF
Dissolve 2 tablespoons instant espresso powder in ¼ cup hot water. Add 3 tablespoons to the base mixture instead of the orange, and 1 tablespoon in with the cocoa when you make the chocolate cake. Omit the orange zest from the topping, and you could melt coffee-flavored chocolate, if you like.

Cherry-Almond Streusel Slice

Preparation time: 20 minutes, or longer if you make your own pastry
Baking time: 40–45 minutes
Cuts into 15 or 18 bars

Cherries and almonds are a classic pairing, but I've tried this with raspberries, sliced apple, and chunks of stone fruit (such as apricots or peach) too, each with great results. The contrast between the rich almond cake, pie crust, and fruit is what makes this irresistible.

For the base and streusel topping
1 recipe sweet basic pie dough, made with all butter (page 210 and Tip), or use 12 oz store-bought

For the cake layer
½ cup all-purpose flour, plus extra for dusting
1¾ sticks (¾ cup plus 2 tbsp) soft butter
1 cup sugar
4 eggs
½ –1 tsp almond extract (depending how almondy you like things)
1 cup almond meal
½ tsp baking powder
¼ tsp salt
½ cup cherry or raspberry jam
1½ cups whole cherries, or ¾ cup pitted (fresh, canned, or frozen and thawed)
a handful of sliced almonds

For the icing (optional)
⅔ cup confectioners' sugar
2–3 tsp lemon juice

1

Preheat the oven to 350°F and put a flat baking sheet in the oven to heat up. Cut one sixth of the dough from the block and set it aside in the fridge—this will be used for the topping later. Roll out the rest on a lightly floured surface until it is just bigger than the base of a 9-inch square pan, then trim it to neaten the edges. Keep any trimmings to use later, and chill these too.

ALL-BUTTER PASTRY
For a deliciously buttery crust you can use 1 stick plus 1 tablespoon butter to make the pastry on page 210, instead of the butter and vegetable shortening.

2

Push the pastry into the pan, letting it come a little way up the sides to make a rim of about ½ inch. If the pastry rips at all, just pinch it back together.

3

To make the cake layer, put the butter and sugar in a large bowl and beat together until creamy and paler. Don't worry about incorporating too much air—a wooden spoon is fine. Add the eggs, almond extract, and almond meal, then beat until combined.

4

Mix the flour, baking powder, and salt in a bowl, then sift it onto the batter. Stir it in until smooth.

5

Spread the jam over the pastry, then spread the cake batter on top. It doesn't matter if some of it spills over the top of the pastry and touches the side of the pan.

6

Remove the pits from the cherries, if using fresh ones (use a knife or cherry pitter, or just press the pits out with your fingers). Cut them in half. Now sprinkle the fruit over the cake, then tear the reserved pastry and trimmings over it to make a struesel top. Scatter with the sliced almonds.

7

Carefully slide the pan onto the baking sheet in the oven. This will give a boost of heat to the bottom of the pan, helping the pastry base to cook thoroughly. Bake for 40–45 minutes, or until the cake has risen to the center, is firm, and a deep, glowing gold. Let cool in the pan. Once cooled, top with the icing. Sift the confectioners' sugar and slowly stir in enough lemon juice to make a smooth, flowing icing, then drizzle liberally over the cake, letting it run off the spoon.

8

Let the icing set, then cut into 15 or 18 bars. It will keep in an airtight container in a cool place for 3 days.

BAKEWELL TART

For bakers with a taste for British classics, line a 9-inch fluted tart pan with the pastry, taking it right to the top of the pan (see page 194 for how to line a pan with pastry). Fill with the jam, batter, and fruit, then scatter with the almonds. Bake as above, then drizzle with the icing and cut into wedges when cooled. Use halved glacé cherries instead of fresh fruit for the full effect.

Carrot Cake with Cream Cheese Frosting

Preparation time: 30 minutes,
plus cooling
Baking time: 30–35 minutes
Makes 12 slices

Carrot cake is perfect as a first cake to make, since it's not only tasty, but also less likely to overcook and be dry, thanks to the water content in the carrots. If you'd like to make the cake in squares or cupcakes instead of layers, see the variations on page 94.

For the cake

1 cup pecans

¾ cup vegetable oil, plus extra
   for greasing

2 cups all-purpose flour

2 tsp baking powder

½ tsp baking soda

2 tsp pumpkin pie spice

½ tsp salt

1 packed cup light brown sugar

1 orange

3 eggs

10 oz carrots

½ cup raisins

For the frosting

1 stick (½ cup) soft butter

10 oz full-fat cream cheese, cold

½ tsp vanilla extract

1 cup confectioners' sugar

1

Preheat the oven to 350°F. Spread the nuts over a baking sheet and cook for 8–10 minutes, or until golden and toasty. Cool, then roughly chop. Toasting nuts will add an extra depth of flavor to the batter, but if you're in a hurry, just chop the nuts and use them as they are.

2

While you wait, get everything else ready. Grease two 8-inch round cake pans with removable bottoms with a little oil, then line the bottoms with parchment paper. Mix the flour, baking powder, baking soda, spices, and salt, then sift into a large bowl. Add the sugar and work it in with your fingers, breaking up any larger lumps, until evenly blended. Finely grate the zest of the orange into the bowl. Squeeze the juice for later.

HOW TO MIX YOUR SPICES
To make your own pumpkin pie spice, combine 1 tablespoon ground cinnamon, 2 teaspoons ground ginger, and ½ teaspoon ground nutmeg. You'll have some left over for next time, too.

3

Crack the eggs into the measuring cup with the oil, add 2 tablespoons orange juice and beat together.

4

Coarsely grate the carrots and measure them to make sure you have 2½ cups. Pour the oil mixture into the dry ingredients and beat until smooth. Add most of the nuts, then the carrots and raisins, and stir until evenly blended. If the batter seems at all stiff, add 1 tablespoon more orange juice. Divide the batter between the prepared pans.

5

Bake for 30–35 minutes, or until the cakes are golden and have risen, and a skewer inserted into the center comes out clean. Cool in the pans on a rack for 10 minutes, then turn out of the pans and cool completely.

6

To make the frosting, put the butter in a large bowl and beat well until creamy and totally smooth. Add the cream cheese and vanilla and beat until smooth and evenly blended. Now sift in the confectioners' sugar and work it in gently with a spatula.

FOR PERFECT FROSTING

It's important that the butter and cream cheese are the correct temperatures, or the frosting can end up lumpy. If that happens, pass it through a sieve and no one will be any the wiser. Do not overwork it once the sugar has been added, as this can loosen the texture.

7

Put one of the cakes upside down on a serving plate, then use an icing spatula to spread about a third of the frosting across it. Top with the other cake, then spread the remaining frosting over the top and the sides (see page 136 for guidance).

8

Sprinkle the reserved pecans over the top. The cake benefits from a little while in the fridge to settle. If it's a hot day, keep it there until you are ready to slice it.

CARROT SHEET CAKE

Use a 9 x 13-inch pan and bake for 40 minutes, or until a skewer comes out clean. Frost, then cut into squares.

CARROT CUPCAKES

Also makes 18 cupcakes. Bake for 20–25 minutes, then cool and frost.

Fudgy Cheesecake Brownies

Preparation time: 20 minutes
Baking time: 30–35 minutes
Makes 16

A swirl of cheesecake topping gives
these brownies a different look,
and a delicious, creamy contrast
to the dark fudginess beneath.
Prefer a simple brownie? Just leave
out the cheesecake topping and
jump to step 8. And yes, the batter
will give that shiny, papery crust
we all love. Turn the page for more
flavor options.

For the brownies

1¾ sticks (¾ cup plus 2 tbsp) butter,
    plus extra for greasing
7 oz bittersweet chocolate, about
    60% cocoa solids (see Tip)
4 eggs
1½ cups sugar
1 cup all-purpose flour
½ cup cocoa powder
½ tsp salt

For the cheesecake topping

7 oz full-fat cream cheese,
    room temperature
1 egg
2 tbsp sugar
1 tsp vanilla extract

1

Grease a 9-inch square cake pan with a little butter, then line it with parchment paper. Preheat the oven to 350°F. Make the brownie base first. Melt the butter in a medium saucepan. While you wait, break the chocolate into pieces, then add them to the melted butter, and take the pan off the heat.

CHOCOLATE IN COOKING
A good-quality 70% cocoa chocolate is often used for baking for its intense cocoa flavor. But it can sometimes seem a little sour and overwhelm a family-style treat like a brownie. My preference is to use a bittersweet chocolate of around 60% cocoa, or a half-and-half mixture of 70% and 50%. This reduces the cost a little, too.

2

Let the chocolate melt until smooth, stirring now and again with a spatula.

3

Put the eggs and sugar in a large bowl. Using a whisk, beat together until frothy and a little thicker, just for 30 seconds or so.

4

Pour the melted butter and chocolate into the eggs and whisk to combine. Put the flour, cocoa, and salt in a sieve, then sift into the bowl.

5

Beat together using your (already chocolatey) whisk, until smooth and thick. Scoop ⅓ cup of the batter from the bowl and set aside, then scrape the rest into the prepared pan and smooth the top.

6

Now make the topping. Put the cream cheese in a large bowl, add the egg, sugar, and vanilla. Whisk until smooth and creamy.

7

Spoon the cheese over the brownie batter in the pan, then spread it into a thin layer using the back of the spoon or a spatula. Spoon the reserved brownie batter over the cheesecake topping. Drag a skewer or the tip of a knife through the cheesecake layer to create feathery swirls.

8

Bake for 30–35 minutes, or until the brownie has risen all over and jiggles just a little in the center when you gently shake the pan. This is vital for a fudgy result. Let cool completely in the pan, then cut into squares. They'll keep in an airtight container for several days.

VARIATIONS
Add different flavors at step 5, and leave out the cheesecake topping.

Classic Walnut Brownies: Fold 1 cup chopped walnuts into the batter.

Sour Cherry & White Chocolate Brownies: Fold in ½ cup dried cherries and ⅓ cup chopped white chocolate.

Peanut Butter Brownies: Warm 4 tablespoons peanut butter in a pan, then spoon it over the raw batter and swirl in with a knife.

Lemon-Glazed Ginger Cake

Preparation time: 20 minutes
Baking time: 50 minutes
Makes 12 slices

Everyone who tried this cake fell in love with it, including me! Making cakes this way with molasses or treacle guarantees a deliciously dense and sticky cake, which keeps very well in an airtight container for at least a week. Don't worry if you don't have a bundt pan—see the instructions for making it in a regular 9 x 13-inch pan over the page.

For the cake
¾ cup vegetable oil, plus extra
    for greasing
¾ cup crystallized ginger
    (or use glacé ginger packed
    in syrup, drained)
1½ packed cups dark brown sugar
½ cup dark molasses or
    black treacle
1 cup milk
3 eggs
1 lemon
2⅓ cups all-purpose flour
1½ tsp baking soda
1 tbsp ground ginger
1 tsp ground allspice
    (or use cinnamon)
¼ tsp salt

For the glaze
1 cup confectioners' sugar
about 2 tbsp lemon juice

1

Preheat the oven to 350°F and grease a 12-cup bundt pan with a little oil, or use nonstick cooking spray. Chop the crystallized ginger into small pieces.

2

Put the dark brown sugar, molasses or treacle, and milk in a large pan and let them melt gently together.

3

Take the pan off the heat, whisk in the oil to cool the mixture, then add the eggs and whisk until smooth. Finely grate in the zest of the lemon.

4

Mix the flour, baking soda, spices, and salt, then sift into a large bowl. Make a well in the center by pushing the flour to the sides of the bowl, then pour in the wet ingredients. Add most of the chopped ginger, saving some for decoration later.

5

Mix the dry ingredients into the wet, going slowly at first. Once everything is mixed, give the batter a good beat with the whisk until smooth and evenly blended. Pour into the prepared bundt pan.

6

Bake for 35 minutes, by which point the cake should have risen all over and be dark golden; but don't open the oven door yet or it will sink. Turn the oven down to 325°F for a final 15 minutes of cooking. Test by inserting a skewer into the deepest part of the cake; it should come out clean. Put the pan on a wire rack and let the cake cool completely.

7

To decorate the cake, sift the confectioners' sugar into a large bowl. Squeeze the lemon juice, then stir 4–5 teaspoons into the sugar until smooth. It needs to be thicker than you think, so see how it flows from the spoon before you add any more juice. Turn the cake out onto a serving plate, then drizzle with the icing.

8

Scatter the reserved chopped ginger over the cake, then let the icing set for at least 30 minutes.

NO BUNDT PAN?
No problem, simply make gingerbread fingers instead. Bake the cake in the same way, in a parchment-lined 9 x 13-inch baking pan, until a skewer inserted into the center comes out clean. Drizzle with the glaze, or make a double batch with 2 cups sugar and a few more teaspoons of lemon juice, then spread it thickly over the top of the cake. Let set, then cut into bars, wiping the knife clean before making each cut.

Skinny Blueberry Muffins

Preparation time: 15 minutes
Baking time: 25 minutes
Makes 12 muffins

Muffins are easy to grab and go, but I always want something with at least a nod to health in the morning. This butter-less, fluffy muffin is good enough to rival the one from the coffee shop, without the guilt trip. The sweetness from the apple reduces the amount of sugar and fat needed, and there's added fibre from the fruit and flour, too.

For the muffins

1 lemon

1 cup milk

1 medium dessert apple

1⅔ cups all-purpose flour

1 cup whole-wheat flour

1 tsp baking powder

1 tsp baking soda

1 tsp pumpkin pie spice

½ tsp salt

½ packed cup light brown sugar

⅓ cup vegetable oil

2 tsp vanilla extract

2 eggs

1 cup blueberries (fresh are best
   but frozen are fine)

For the glaze (optional)

⅓ cup confectioners' sugar

2–3 tsp milk

1
Preheat the oven to 400°F and line a 12-cup muffin pan with paper liners. Grate the zest from the lemon (save this for later), then squeeze the juice from one half. Stir 1 tablespoon juice into the milk and let stand for a few minutes until it thickens and turns a bit lumpy.

2
Meanwhile, grate the apple with a coarse grater, skin and all.

3
Mix the flours, baking powder, baking soda, spice, and salt, then sift into a large bowl. This allows for the rising agents to be thoroughly mixed with the flour. Return the bran from the whole-wheat flour, which will collect in the sieve, to the bowl. Stir in the sugar, then make a well in the middle. Beat the oil, vanilla, and eggs into the now-lumpy milk.

4

Pour the liquid into the well. Add the apple and berries too.

5

Stir the mixture together briefly to make a rough batter. Don't worry if there are still a few bits of dry flour here and there.

6

Spoon generous heaping spoons of batter into the lined pan, or use an ice cream scoop, which helps do the job very cleanly; about one scoop per liner. They will seem quite full, but that's fine. Bake for about 25 minutes, or until they have risen well and are golden. Don't open the oven until every muffin has risen right to the center.

7

Make the glaze, if you like. Sift the confectioners' sugar into a bowl, then slowly beat in the milk, to make a smooth paste. Stir in the lemon zest. Drizzle the glaze over the muffins and let cool.

GET AHEAD

Muffins are always best baked fresh, so why not bag the wet ingredients, including the apple, and chill. Get the dry ingredients ready in a bowl. In the morning, combine the two mixtures and get the muffins in the oven in 2 minutes flat.

CHEESE & HAM CORNBREAD MUFFINS

For a quick savory option, switch the whole-wheat flour for fine cornmeal. Use only 1 teaspoon sugar and omit the vanilla, spice, and fruit. Beat 2 teaspoons wholegrain mustard into the soured milk, egg, and ¼ cup oil. Stir in ½ cup grated hard cheese such as Cheddar, ½ cup chopped cooked ham, and ½ cup canned sweetcorn. Bake for 18 minutes.

Fruity Granola Bars

Preparation time: 20 minutes
Baking time: 35 minutes
Makes 12 bars

These satisfying bars are packed with good things to keep you going until lunchtime, and the butter and sugar have been kept to a minimum with no loss of texture or flavor. The recipe can be easily changed to include your favorite dried fruit, nuts, and seeds. Quick-cooking rolled oats are the best choice for these bars because they stick together nicely.

2½ cups quick-cooking rolled oats

½ cup unsweetened desiccated
   coconut

½ cup pumpkin or sunflower seeds

½ cup sliced almonds

½ stick (¼ cup) butter, plus
   extra for greasing

½ packed cup light brown sugar

a pinch of salt

½ cup honey

½ cup soft dried apricots

2 tbsp fruit juice (apple works well),
   or use water

1 cup mixed dried berries and
   cherries (or use raisins or other
   dried fruit)

1

Preheat the oven to 325°F. Mix the oats, coconut, seeds, and nuts on a large baking sheet and bake for 15 minutes, stirring half way through, until they smell toasty and are pale golden here and there. Meanwhile, grease a 9-inch square baking pan, then line it with parchment paper. Put the butter, sugar, salt, and honey in a large saucepan and melt them gently together to make a syrup. Chop the dried apricots, or snip them with scissors.

2

Pour the toasted oats, seeds, and nuts into the pan, then add the fruit juice or water and the dried fruit. Stir well with a spatula until everything is evenly coated in the syrup. Press the granola into the baking pan and smooth it flat with the back of a spoon.

3

Bake for 35 minutes, or until golden all over, then let cool completely in the pan. Lift the baked slab of granola from the pan using the paper to help, then cut into bars using a large sharp knife. Re-wrap in clean parchment paper and keep in the pan or an airtight container for up to 1 week.

Caramel & Walnut Coffee Cake

Preparation time: 25 minutes,
plus cooling
Baking time: 20–25 minutes
Makes 12 slices

A stalwart of British teashops and
coffee mornings, this cake deserves
a place in cake-lovers' hearts
everywhere. I like to moisten
the layers with strong coffee and
finish with a crown of caramelized
walnuts and frosting for a slightly
flashier riff on the original.

For the cake
2 tbsp instant espresso,
    or ½ cup very strong coffee
2¼ sticks (1 cup plus 2 tbsp)
    soft butter, plus extra for greasing
½ cup walnut halves
1¼ cups sugar, preferably superfine,
    plus 2 tbsp extra
5 eggs, room temperature
2 tbsp milk
2⅓ cups all-purpose flour
1 tbsp baking powder
¼ tsp salt

For the frosting and decoration
½ cup sugar (optional)
½ cup walnut halves
1 tbsp instant espresso
    (or 1 tbsp very strong coffee)
1 stick (½ cup) soft butter
2¼ cups confectioners' sugar
1 tbsp maple syrup (optional)

1

2

3

4

5

1

Preheat the oven to 350°F. If using instant espresso, dissolve it in ½ cup just-boiled water and set it aside to cool. Use a little butter to grease two 8-inch round cake pans with removable bottoms, then line the bottoms with parchment paper. Finely chop the nuts.

2

Put the butter and sugar for the cake in a large bowl and beat with an electric mixer until creamy and pale. Crack in the eggs and add the milk. Mix the flour, baking powder, and salt together, sift them over the eggs, then beat together until creamy.

3

Using a spatula or large spoon, fold in the chopped walnuts and 5 tablespoons of the cooled coffee.

4

Spoon the batter into the prepared pans and level the tops. Bake for 20–25 minutes, or until it has risen, is golden, springs back to the touch, and a skewer inserted in the center comes out clean.

5

Let cool in the pans for 10 minutes, then turn onto a cooling rack. I like to peel the paper from the underneath, put this on the rack cake-side down, then put the cake on top of it, bottom-side up. This prevents the cakes from sticking to the rack. Stir the extra sugar into the remaining coffee, let it dissolve, then drizzle this all over the cakes. Let cool completely.

6

The frosting and topping can be simple, or less so, it's up to you. If you want the simple option, jump straight to step 8, use plain walnuts and add 1 tablespoon maple syrup to the recipe instead of using the caramel. Or, if you're with me on the caramel, read on: Line a baking sheet with parchment. Put the sugar in a small saucepan or small deep frying pan, and heat gently. It will start to look patchy here and there. Don't be tempted to stir it at this point or it could seize, becoming hard and opaque.

7

Carefully swirl the melted patches of sugar over the dry bits, returning to the heat occasionally, to make an even-colored dark coppery caramel. If there are few bits of sugar left, now you can give it a quick stir. Put the whole walnuts in the caramel, then use a fork to transfer them one by one to the lined sheet to harden. When you've finished, add 1 tablespoon water to the pan and let it bubble to a runny, dark caramel.

8

If using instant espresso for the frosting, dissolve it in 1 tablespoon just-boiled water. Beat the butter until creamy, then gradually work in the confectioners' sugar. Once all the dry sugar has disappeared, give it a good whizz until pale and fluffy. Add the coffee and 1 tablespoon of the caramel (or maple syrup), then beat again.

9

Spread the frosting on the top of each cake, stack them on a serving plate, and top with the walnuts. The cake will keep well in an airtight container for 3 days or so. The layers can be frozen for up to a month, and the frosting and nuts can be made a few days in advance.

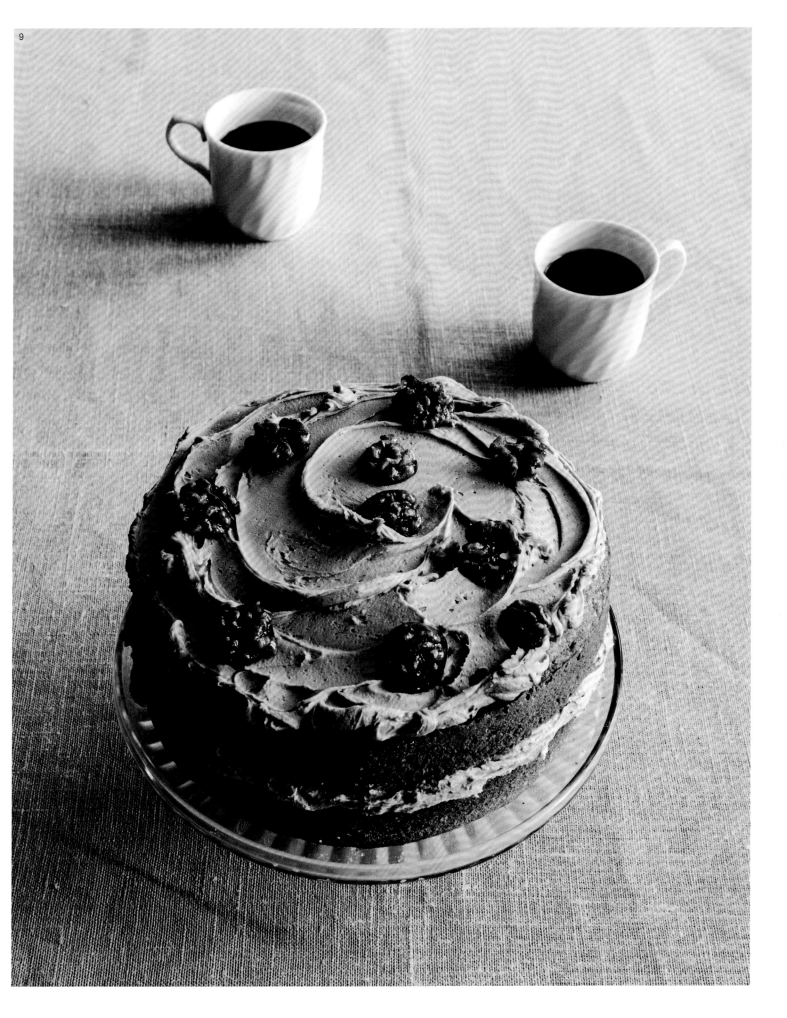

Blueberry-Cinnamon Crumb Cake

Preparation time: 30 minutes
Baking time: 35 minutes
Makes 16 squares

Great cakes for coffee time, these
little fruity squares are also prime
candidates for dessert, served
just-warm with a splash of cream.
The batter, made with buttermilk,
is tender and light and will
accommodate just about any fruit
you want to add; turn the page for
some ideas.

For the cake

½ stick plus 3 tbsp (¼ cup plus
   3 tbsp) soft butter, plus extra
   for greasing

¾ cup sugar

1⅔ cups all-purpose flour

1 tsp baking powder

½ tsp baking soda

¼ tsp salt

2 eggs, room temperature

1 tsp vanilla extract

½ cup buttermilk (or use runny
   low-fat natural yogurt)

1 tbsp milk

For the fruit layers and crumb

1 tbsp plus 1 tsp cinnamon

¼ cup turbinado sugar

2 cups blueberries, fresh or frozen
   and defrosted

⅓ cup all-purpose flour

a pinch of salt

2 tbsp butter, room temperature

1 tsp confectioners' sugar (optional)

1

Preheat the oven to 350°F. Grease a 9-inch square cake pan with butter, then line it with parchment paper. Put the butter and sugar in a large bowl and beat with an electric mixer until fluffy and light.

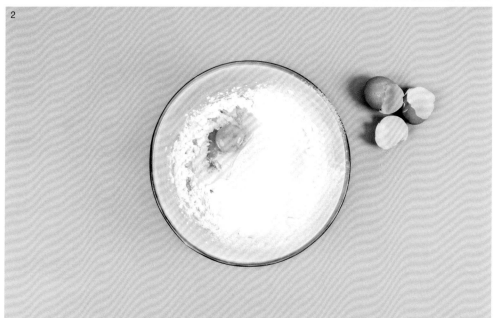

2

Mix the flour, baking powder, baking soda, and salt, then sift them into the bowl. Add the eggs and vanilla.

3

Beat everything together until smooth, then beat in the buttermilk and milk to make a smooth, creamy mixture.

4

Spoon half the batter into the prepared pan. Mix 1 tablespoon cinnamon and 2 tablespoons turbinado sugar, then scatter half of this over the cake, followed by half the berries. Repeat the layers.

KEEP THEM SEPARATED
For defined layers, take care when spreading the second layer of cake batter over the blueberries, as they'll try and come along for the ride with the spatula. This will stop once you get going.

5

Make the crumb topping. Put the flour, salt, remaining cinnamon, and turbinado sugar in a bowl. Cut the butter into small pieces, add them to the flour, then rub together until it looks like fine crumbs. When ready, squish some of the crumbs together to make big, cookie-dough-like clumps.

6

Sprinkle the crumbs over the top of the cake, then bake for 35 minutes, or until it has risen all the way to the center, looks golden, and the crumb topping is crisp. Cool in the pan for 15 minutes, then lift out the cake using the lining paper and let cool on a rack.

7

Dust the cake with a little confectioners' sugar if you like, then cut it into squares to serve.

PEACH CRUMB CAKE
Replace the berries with 2 chopped ripe peaches.

APPLE & PECAN CRUMB CAKE
Thinly slice a tangy, sweet apple (to make 1 cup), mix with ½ cup chopped pecans, then layer as before. A few blobs of cream cheese added here and there would also make a tasty change.

Seriously Chocolatey Cookies

Preparation time: 10 minutes
Baking time: 10 minutes per batch
Makes 20

It's hard to please everyone when it comes to cookies, but here's my idea of cookie heaven: a crisp outer shell, soft inside, and a bit of chewy resistance thanks to the bittersweet molasses. They're perfect for ice-cream cookie sandwiches, too. The most important thing is not to bake them for longer than the times given.

---

6 oz bittersweet chocolate,
   60% cocoa solids
¾ stick (¼ cup plus 2 tbsp) butter
2 eggs
1 packed cup dark brown sugar
1 generous tbsp black treacle
   or dark molasses
1 tsp vanilla extract
1½ cups all-purpose flour
1 tbsp good-quality cocoa powder
½ tsp baking powder
¼ tsp salt
⅓ cup semi-sweet chocolate chips
   or chopped chocolate, to stir
   through and sprinkle on top
3½ oz white chocolate (optional)

1
Preheat the oven to 350°F and line one or two baking sheets with parchment paper. Roughly chop the chocolate and put it in a heatproof bowl with the butter, then melt until smooth.

MELTING CHOCOLATE
Place the bowl over a pan of barely simmering water (the bowl should be just larger than the rim of the pan, so that it sits happily on top), making sure it doesn't touch the water. Let the chocolate melt for about 5 minutes, stirring once or twice, until smooth throughout. Alternatively, microwave on high in 20-second bursts, stirring after each one, until smooth. It's important to use a heatproof bowl, such as Pyrex, otherwise it can become very hot and scorch the chocolate.

2
Separate one of the eggs (see page 127), then put the yolk, the whole egg, sugar, molasses, and vanilla in a large bowl. Beat with a whisk or an electric mixer for about 1 minute, or until the mixture becomes smooth and a little paler.

3
Beat in the melted chocolate and butter.

4
Mix the flour, cocoa, baking powder, and salt in a bowl, then sift them over the chocolate mixture. Stir together to make a soft dough, then stir in all but 1 heaping tablespoon of the chocolate chips, if using.

5

Spoon heaping tablespoons of dough onto the lined sheets, leaving room for the cookies to spread. Press the remaining chocolate chips on top of the cookies. You'll find that the longer you leave the dough, the firmer it becomes, but this is fine.

6

Bake the cookies for 10 minutes for very soft centers and crisp edges (they will rise, but still feel very soft when pressed in the middle), or 12 minutes for a chewier result. Remove from the oven, let them firm up for a couple of minutes on the sheet, then carefully lift onto a cooling rack and let cool completely.

Melt the white chocolate, if using, following the same method as before. Take extra care not to overheat it, as white chocolate will burn easily. Drizzle it over the cookies and let set.

7

The cookies are ready to eat as soon as the white chocolate sets, or they will keep in an airtight container for up to 3 days.

VARIATIONS
Try folding a handful of roughly chopped macadamia nuts through the dough at the same time as, or instead of, the chocolate chips. You can add milk or white chocolate chunks if you like; spices, such as ¼ teaspoon crushed cardamom seeds; raisins; or perhaps a sprinkling of crushed peppermint candy on top before baking for a Christmas twist. ½ teaspoon of freshly ground black pepper adds warmth to the cookies, if you're making them for grown-ups. Add it with the flour (thanks to Liz, one of our photographers, for the tip).

Maple-Pecan Cinnamon Rolls

Preparation time: 40 minutes,
plus rising and proofing time
Baking time: 30–35 minutes
Makes 8 large or 12 smaller rolls

Richly spiced and nutty, this version
of my favorite sticky cinnamon rolls
is just the right side of sweet, thanks
to a layer of cream cheese hidden
inside. The cardamom will bring
the wonderful scent of Scandinavian
baking to your kitchen.

For the dough

½ stick (¼ cup) butter, plus extra
    for greasing
½ cup plus 2 tbsp milk
2 eggs
3½ cups bread flour, plus extra
    for kneading
2 tsp instant dry yeast
¼ cup sugar, preferably superfine
1 tsp salt

For the filling and to finish

1½ cups pecans
5 cardamom pods
1–2 tsp ground cinnamon,
    to your taste
2 tbsp sugar
¼ cup plus 3 tbsp maple syrup
9 oz full-fat cream cheese,
    room temperature

1

Melt the butter in a small pan, then using a fork, beat in the milk, followed by the eggs. Sift all the dry ingredients together, then make a well in the center.

2

Pour the wet ingredients into the dry ones, then mix with a wooden spoon to make a rough and fairly sticky dough. Leave for 5 minutes.

3

Dust the work surface with flour, then turn the dough out onto it. Start kneading, flouring the dough and your hands if you need to, but avoid adding too much. If the dough sticks a lot, scrape away any bits with a knife, wash and dry your hands and start again, dusting the work surface, the dough and your hands with more flour. After 5–10 minutes, when the dough feels very smooth and springy, put it in an oiled food storage bag or bowl, cover and let rise in a warm place for 1 hour, or until doubled in size.

4

Make the filling while you wait. Finely chop the pecans (use a food processor if you have one). Bash the cardamom pods to release their seeds, discard the husks, then grind the seeds finely with a mortar and pestle. Mix the nuts, spices, sugar, and ¼ cup maple syrup.

5

Flour the work surface again, then turn the risen dough out onto it. Sprinkle with a little flour, then press it out to a rectangle, about 10 x 12 inches. Spread the cream cheese all over it, going right to the edges. Scatter with the pecan mixture, then roll into a tight sausage, starting from a long edge for 12 rolls, or a short edge for 8 rolls. If it looks a bit uneven, pat the dough to straighten things up.

6

Cut the sausage into 8 or 12 slices with a large non-serrated knife dusted with flour (the flour helps stop the dough sticking).

7

Generously grease a pan with butter (a 9-inch round for 8 rolls, or a 9 x 13-inch rectangle for 12), then tuck the slices into it. Keep the seam of each spiral facing inwards. If the spirals have squashed a bit during slicing, pat them into shape before they go into the pan.

8

Cover loosely with oiled plastic wrap or a food storage bag, then let proof in a warm place for 30 minutes, or until risen. Poke the dough lightly; once ready, it will not spring back. Preheat the oven to 400°F.

9

Bake for 10 minutes, then turn the oven down to 350°F and bake for another 20–25 minutes (depending on the size of your rolls), or until they have risen, are golden all over, and cooked right through. If you're unsure, carefully turn the rolls upside down out of their pan and tap sharply in the middle of the dough. It should give a hollow sound, and also be a good golden brown color.

10

Brush the rolls with more maple syrup and enjoy the same day.

HOT CROSS BUNS OR TEACAKES
Add 2 teaspoons pumpkin pie spice to the flour and use scant ½ cup sugar. Knead in 1 cup dried fruit at the end of step 3 and let rise. Omit the filling. Shape into 12 balls, let proof, then slash each roll with a cross shape, brush with beaten egg, and bake. Brush with a little corn or golden syrup once out of the oven. Serve split, toasted, and buttered.

Easy Baked Doughnuts

Preparation time: 30 minutes,
plus rising and proofing
Baking time: 10–12 minutes per batch
Makes 8–10 doughnuts

A very convincing doughnut is totally
possible without any deep-frying.
The secret is to make a very soft,
buttery dough that is shaped while
very cold. If cinnamon doughnuts are
your favorite, add ½ teaspoon to the
sugar. If you like them with jam, just
dunk them in. The dough can also be
glazed with beaten egg to make light
brioche rolls, if you prefer.

For the dough

1 stick (½ cup) butter

¾ cup milk

2 eggs

2 cups all-purpose flour,
    plus extra for shaping

1½ tsp instant dry yeast

¼ cup sugar

¼ tsp salt

oil, for greasing

For 10 sugared doughnuts

1 stick (½ cup) butter

¾ cup superfine sugar

For 10 glazed doughnuts

1⅔ cups confectioners' sugar

5 tbsp milk

1 tsp vanilla extract

For 10 thickly iced doughnuts

1⅔ cups confectioners' sugar

¼ cup milk

1 tsp vanilla extract

a few drops of food coloring

2 tbsp sprinkles

1

Gently melt the butter in the milk in a pan, then remove from the heat. Let it cool for a few minutes. Meanwhile, separate the eggs. Put the flour in a large bowl and add the yeast, sugar, and salt.

SEPARATING EGGS
Gently crack the egg shell against the side of a small bowl. Slowly pull the shell apart as cleanly as possible along the crack, and pour the yolk into one half of the shell, letting the white drain into the bowl below. Pass the yolk into the other half shell to allow more white to drain away. Drop the yolk into a separate bowl. Take care not to pierce the yolk.

2

Mix the buttery milk and the yolks into the dry ingredients, to make a very wet dough, almost a batter.

3

Now comes the fun part: Hold the bowl steady with one hand, then with the other, pull up as much dough as you can, then let it go, so that it slaps back into the bowl. Do this for about 5 minutes, and the dough will turn from very liquid to something with more body, and it will become stretchy and smoother. It will be much looser than regular bread dough, which is why this stage is all done within the safe confines of the bowl. You can do this step with a dough hook in a stand mixer, if you have one.

4

Oil a second bowl or a large food storage bag. Scoop the dough into it, cover the bowl with oiled plastic wrap or seal the bag, then chill for at least 4 hours, or until firm. Overnight is ideal. It won't double in size like bread dough usually does.

5

Have 2 large baking sheets ready, lined with parchment. Flour the work surface, then turn the dough out of the bowl. Dust it with flour, cut it in half, and put one half in the fridge to keep cold. Shape the doughnuts in one of 3 ways, then repeat with the rest of the dough:

1) For classic ring doughnuts, roll the dough out to about ½ inch thick. Stamp the dough into circles with a 3½ or 4-inch cutter, then remove the middle sections with a smaller cutter (I use my trusty egg cup). If it's your first time handling this kind of dough, I'd stick to this shape for now. Place the trimmings on top of each other, then roll again until ½ inch thick and repeat. Try not to knead the dough, as it will become springy or too warm.

2) For twists, roll the dough to a 10 x 6-inch rectangle, then cut into strips about 1 inch across. Pinch the ends of 2 pieces together, then twist into a rope. Pinch the other end together. Tuck the ends under to give a neat shape and pinch underneath to secure.

3) For twisted rings, proceed as for 2, but pinch the dough together in a ring shape once it has been twisted.

6
Lift the shapes onto a lined sheet pan, giving the dough plenty of room to rise. Cover loosely with a dish towel or oiled plastic wrap, then leave in a warm place to proof for 30 minutes–1 hour. When you see the dough is growing nicely, preheat the oven to 375°F.

7
When ready to bake, the dough will have grown by about 75 percent. If you push the side of one doughnut and your finger leaves an indent, it's ready. If not, leave them a little longer. At this point, the dough will be very delicate and difficult to move, so if they are rising unevenly, turn the pan around instead of trying to move them individually.

8

Bake for 10–12 minutes, or until dark golden and puffed up. Meanwhile, prepare your glaze, icing, or sugaring ingredients. To prepare for sugared doughnuts, melt the butter in a pan, and have half the superfine sugar spread out in a wide bowl. For glazed doughnuts, sift the confectioners' sugar into a bowl, then gradually mix in the milk and vanilla, until smooth and fairly runny. For iced doughnuts, repeat as above, adding a little food coloring to make a thick paste.

9

For sugared doughnuts, turn the warm doughnuts around in the melted butter, let the excess drip away, then turn in the sugar and let cool. When you've sugared half the doughnuts, discard the sugar, which will be a bit buttery by now, and repeat. For glazed doughnuts, toss one doughnut at a time into the glaze, lift out with the help of 2 forks, let the excess drip away, then let dry on a rack. For iced doughnuts, set them on a rack, spoon the icing over them, and decorate with the sprinkles.

10

Eat the doughnuts on the day they are made. The dough can easily be made a couple of days ahead, or frozen flat on trays once shaped in step 5, then packed into freezer containers and frozen for up to 2 weeks. Spread them out on trays to thaw, then proof and bake.

SPECIAL

BAKES

Chocolate Fudge
Layer Cake

Preparation time: 30 minutes,
plus cooling
Baking time: 30 minutes
Makes 12 slices

If you need any persuading to make
this yummy cake, let me tell you it's
a simple stir-together method using
just two pans. The frosting is dead
easy, and the whole thing keeps
well. A go-to cake for birthdays,
Easter (with chocolate eggs on top),
or any time you need a nice piece
of good old gooey chocolate cake.

For the cake

1¼ sticks (½ cup plus 2 tbsp) butter,
   plus extra for greasing
2¾ cups all-purpose flour
¼ cup plus 2 tbsp cocoa powder
1 tsp baking soda
2 tsp baking powder
¼ tsp salt
1½ cups light brown sugar
1¼ cups milk
½ cup plus 2 tbsp vegetable oil
1 tsp vanilla extract

For the chocolate frosting

14-oz can sweetened
   condensed milk
½ cup plus 2 tbsp heavy cream
7 oz bittersweet chocolate, 50, 60
   or 70% cocoa solids, depending
   on your taste
½ stick (¼ cup) butter
1 tsp vanilla extract

134

1
Preheat the oven to 350°F. Put the butter in a saucepan and melt it gently. Meanwhile, use a little extra butter to grease two 8-inch round cake pans with removable bottoms, then line the bottoms with circles of parchment paper.

2
Mix together the flour, cocoa, baking soda, baking powder, and salt, then sift into a large bowl.

3
Add the sugar and break up any lumps. Make a well in the center, pushing the mixture out to the sides of the bowl. Whisk the milk, oil, and vanilla into the melted butter.

4
Pour the wet ingredients into the well. Using a whisk, slowly mix the ingredients together. Once everything is mixed, give it a good beating with the whisk until smooth and evenly blended. Using a spatula, divide the batter equally between the pans and spread it flat.

5
Bake for 30 minutes, or until the cakes have risen, are firm and slightly shrunken from the sides of the pans. Let cool in the pans for 10 minutes, then turn out onto a cooling rack and cool completely. If you want to get ahead, wrap and store the cakes for up to 3 days once cooled, or freeze for up to 1 month.

6
To make the frosting, put the condensed milk and cream in a saucepan and stir it over low heat until it starts to bubble at the edges. Take care and keep stirring, as it can easily stick on the bottom. Break up the chocolate into squares while you wait, then chop it fairly small. Cut the butter into cubes.

7

Remove the pan from the heat, add the chocolate, butter, and vanilla, then let melt, stirring now and again. It will thicken as it cools. Beat it occasionally, until thick and fudgy and completely cooled.

8

For a four-layer cake, you'll need to cut each cake in half horizontally. You might find this easier if you chill the cake for 30 minutes beforehand.

CUTTING WITH EASE
With a large serrated knife, score a line around the "waist" of the cake, cutting about 1 inch in. Turn the cake with one hand and keep the knife in the other. Keep a steady hand, and the start and finish points should meet up. Cut the cake using gentle sweeps of the knife, keeping it parallel with the surface. Rotate the cake a few degrees after each cut. You will soon reach the middle and the top half will be freed. Repeat with the second cake. If the layers end up a bit uneven after cutting, don't worry—the frosting will hide it.

9

Sandwich the cakes together on a serving plate, using just under ½ cup frosting between each layer. I like to put a small dot on the serving plate too, to stop the cake from moving around. Spoon the remaining frosting on top of the cake. Spread it out thickly, then, working on about a quarter of the cake at a time, work it over the edge and down to meet the plate. Try to keep going in one fluid movement. Repeat all over.

10

Smooth and swirl the frosting if you like, or leave it rough. Let the cake sit somewhere cool for an hour before slicing. It can be decorated the day before needed and kept in a cool, dark place.

Linzer Cookies

Preparation time: 15 minutes,
plus chilling
Baking time: 10 minutes per batch
Makes about 22

These lovely cookies are perfect
for giving at Christmas or Valentine's
—although the centers can be cut
into circles, stars, or whatever shape
suits the occasion. The buttery dough
is also a versatile go-to when you
need an elegant cookie to decorate
(think birthdays or baby showers),
or as a crisp bite to counter a creamy,
smooth dessert.

For the cookie dough

1½ sticks (¾ cup) soft butter, plus
    extra for greasing
⅔ cup skinless shelled hazelnuts
    (or use almond meal, see Tip)
½ cup superfine sugar
1 egg
1 tsp vanilla extract
1⅔ cups all-purpose flour,
    plus extra for dusting
¼ tsp salt
½ tsp ground cinnamon
1 small orange, grated zest only
    (optional)

For decorating

1 tbsp confectioners' sugar
¾ cup raspberry jam (or use Nutella
    or lemon curd)

1
Preheat the oven to 350°F. Lightly grease 2 baking sheets with butter, then line them with parchment paper. Put the nuts in a food processor with 1 tablespoon of the sugar, then pulse until finely ground. Pour them into a bowl.

DON'T OVERDO IT
Nuts can quickly turn from finely ground to oily, clumpy, and unusable. Pulsing the blades and using a little sugar should avoid this.

2
Separate the egg (see page 127), then put the yolk in the processor bowl with the remaining sugar, the vanilla, and butter.

3
Process the ingredients together until creamy and evenly mixed.

4
Add the flour, salt, cinnamon, and ground nuts to the processor bowl. Finely grate in the orange zest, if using, then pulse until the ingredients form a soft dough ball. You may need to scrape the sides of the bowl down once or twice.

NO PROCESSOR?
No problem: use ¾ cup plus 2 tablespoons almond meal instead. Beat the yolk, sugar, vanilla, and butter in a large bowl, using a wooden spoon or an electric mixer, until pale and creamy. Work the rest of the ingredients into the mixture using a table knife, then knead briefly to make a smooth dough.

5
Lightly dust the work surface with flour, turn out the dough onto it, then split it into 2 equal balls. Flatten each ball into a saucer-size disk. Wrap in plastic wrap and chill for 20–30 minutes, or until firm but not rock solid.

6

Sprinkle more flour on the work surface, then get ready to roll. Press ridges into one of the disks of dough with a rolling pin (this stretches it without overworking it, which makes it tough). Turn the dough and repeat this ridging a few times, until it is about ¾ inch thick. If any cracks appear, pinch them together. Now roll the dough to about ⅛ inch thick.

7

Using a 2½-inch fluted pastry cutter, stamp out 12 rounds. Next, using a small heart or star-shape cutter (or even the end of a wide icing tube to make a round hole), cut out shapes from the centers of half the cookies.

8

Carefully lift the whole round cookies onto one baking sheet, and the cookies with the holes onto the other. Squish the remains of the dough together (taking care not to knead it, as this can make the dough tough), re-roll, and stamp out more cookies until you have filled the baking sheets.

9

Bake the whole cookies for 10–11 minutes and the cut-out cookies for 9 minutes, or until they are pale golden and smell nutty. Let stand for 2 minutes, then lift onto cooling racks and let cool completely. Repeat with the second batch of dough.

10

Use a fine-mesh sieve to dust the confectioners' sugar over the cut-out cookies. Spoon about 1 teaspoon jam over the whole cookies, then sandwich together with the cut-outs. The cookies will keep in an airtight container for 3–5 days and are best sandwiched on the day you're going to eat them.

Coconut Layer Cake

Preparation time: 45 minutes
Baking time: 25 minutes
Cuts into 12 or 16 very tall pieces

Tall, frosted, and a little over
the top, this cake is built from
coconut sponges alternating with
a silky-smooth coconut meringue
buttercream and lemon curd layers.
It's less sweet then a traditional
Southern-style frosted coconut
cake, but if you prefer it that way
see page 145 for an easy twist.

For the cake layers

½ cup unsweetened desiccated
  finely shredded coconut

2 sticks (1 cup) soft butter

1 cup plus 2 tbsp sugar,
  preferably superfine

1 tsp vanilla extract

5 eggs, room temperature

2½ cups all-purpose flour

1 tbsp baking powder

½ tsp salt

½ cup full-fat coconut milk

To decorate

5 eggs (you will only need
  the whites)

2½ cups confectioners' sugar

a pinch of salt

1 tsp vanilla extract

2 sticks plus 5 tbsp (generous
  1¼ cups) soft butter

½ cup full-fat coconut milk

1 cup good-quality lemon curd

2½ cups toasted coconut chips

1
Soak the desiccated coconut in boiling water for 15 minutes (or longer if you can), then pour it into a sieve and press out the excess water. Use a little of the butter to grease two 8-inch round cake pans with removable bottoms, then line the bottoms with parchment paper. Preheat the oven to 350°F.

2
Using an electric mixer, beat the butter, sugar, and vanilla together until creamy and pale, scraping down the sides of the bowl every now and again with a spatula. Beat in an egg until completely combined, fluffy, and light. Repeat with the other eggs, one by one. If it starts to look at all lumpy, add 1 tablespoon of the flour and it will become smooth again.

3
Thoroughly mix the flour, baking powder, and salt in a bowl. Sift half into the cake batter, then fold it in using a spatula or large metal spoon. Next, fold in the coconut milk, then fold in the rest of the flour mixture, then the drained coconut.

4

Using a spatula, divide the batter evenly between the pans and spread it flat.

TAKE A SHORTCUT
If you're in a rush, the cakes can be made using the all-in-one method (see page 8), adding 1 extra teaspoon baking powder.

5

Bake for 25 minutes, or until the cakes have risen, are firm, and slightly shrunken back from the sides of the pans. Let cool on a rack for 10 minutes, then remove from the pans and let cool completely.

6

For a four-layer cake, you'll need to cut each cake in half horizontally. Use a large serrated knife and score a line first around the "waist" of the cake, then cut through gently and smoothly, rotating the cake after each cut (see page 136 for more details).

NEED MORE PRACTICE?
If your cakes are a bit uneven, don't worry, the frosting will cover it up. Inserting toothpicks into one point of the cake at equal intervals is a great way help re-build the cake layers in their original positions, and avoid an overly uneven result.

7

Clean the mixer thoroughly. For the frosting, bring 2 inches water to a simmer in a medium pan. Separate the eggs, then put the whites into a very clean, large, heatproof bowl (one that will sit just on top of the pan), then sift in the sugar. Add the pinch of salt and beat together until smooth. Sit the bowl on the pan, then beat the whites for about 7 minutes, or until very thick and shiny. It's thick enough when you can stand a teaspoon upright in the bowl without it falling over. Beat in the vanilla.

SEVEN-MINUTE FROSTING
If you prefer to use classic 7-minute frosting as a thick and fluffy cake topping, then it's ready now. It's best spread immediately, then left to set for a while before cutting.

8

Scrape the meringue into another cold bowl, then beat for a few minutes more until just about room temperature. Keep the pan of hot water—it may come in handy in a moment. Beat the soft butter into the meringue, one tablespoon at a time, waiting for each one to disappear completely before adding the next. You will find that the volume of the mixture falls at first, and may seem a little loose, but keep going.

9

The frosting will suddenly change from billowy to silky and thick as you add all the butter. When all the butter has been added, gradually beat in the coconut milk. If the mixture starts to feel a bit lumpy, warm it very gently over the hot water for a few seconds while beating, and it will loosen up again.

MERINGUE BUTTERCREAM

Although more time-consuming than regular buttercream, meringue buttercream is a great one to have up your sleeve for a really luxurious cake frosting. It's also delicious with cooled melted dark chocolate whisked into it, instead of the coconut. Meringue buttercream is very good natured, and can be made a few days in advance, chilled, then re-beaten when ready to use. It pipes super-smoothly too.

10

You're now ready to assemble the cake. Place one layer on a serving plate and spread with ½ cup lemon curd. Top with the second layer of cake, then add 1¼ cups frosting and spread it evenly to the edges. Top the third layer with curd too.

11

Place the final cake layer on top, then spread the remaining frosting all over the cake and smooth it with an icing spatula. Mound it on the top of the cake first, then spread it down and around the cake. Press the coconut chips up the side of the cake and sprinkle them over the top.

TOASTING YOUR OWN COCONUT

Spread the coconut chips over a large, lipped baking sheet. Bake at 350°F for 5 minutes, stirring half way, until tinged with gold here and there.

12

Brush any excess chips from the serving plate. Keep the cake cool until serving. If making ahead, chill the cake, but let it come up to room temperature before eating it.

Pumpkin Pie

Preparation time: 1 hour, including
blind baking, plus chilling
Baking time: 45 minutes
Serves 12

Essential baking for fall, especially
at Thanksgiving, this pie is
delicately set and spiced, with a
good crisp crust. A big dollop of
boozy maple cream on the side
really complements the flavor of
the pumpkin. There's a recipe for
pumpkin pie spice on page 93
if you'd like to make your own.

For the pie crust
1 recipe basic sweet pie dough (see
    page 210), or use 12 oz
    store-bought
all-purpose flour, for rolling

For the filling
3 eggs
½ packed cup light brown sugar
¼ cup sugar
1 tsp vanilla extract
2–3 tsp pumpkin pie spice mix,
    depending how spicy you
    like your pie
½ cup heavy cream
½ cup milk
2 tbsp maple syrup, or 2 tbsp
    more sugar
15-oz can solid-pack pumpkin purée
    (or see Tip)
a pinch of salt

For the cream
½ cup heavy cream
1 tbsp maple syrup
1 tbsp bourbon or whisky

1
Lightly flour the work surface, then roll out the pastry dough until large enough to line a 9-inch pie pan with a lip or a tart pan with removable bottom. Use the pan as a guide for size, and try to keep the pastry as round as you can. See page 193 for full rolling instructions, if needed.

2
You can either use the rolling pin to lift the pastry into the pan, or try this method: dust the top of the pastry with a little flour, then fold it first in half, then into a triangle. Lift it into the dish, then unfold.

3
Press the pastry against the edges of the pan, then trim off the overhanging pastry with a sharp knife. Prick the bottom all over with a fork, right down to the metal. Crimp the edges, if you like, pushing the pastry between your thumb and forefinger to make deep, V-shaped indents. Repeat all the way round, then chill the pie crust for 15 minutes, or longer if you have time.

ANY HOLES?
Don't worry if your pastry tears. Dampen a little of the leftovers and stick it down well to seal the hole.

4
Preheat the oven to 375°F. Put the pan onto a baking sheet. Tear a sheet of foil that's large enough to completely cover the pastry, edges and all. Pour in some pie weights to cover the base, mounding them up a little towards the edges. Bake for 20 minutes.

5

Check under the foil; if the pastry looks dry and set, remove the covering. If not, bake for another 5 minutes. When ready, carefully spoon out the hot pie weights, then remove the foil. Bake for another 15–20 minutes, or until it is golden and feels sandy. If the edges color before the base is ready, cover them with foil.

6

Make the filling while you wait. Beat the eggs, saving 1 tablespoon to glaze the pie shell later. Beat the rest of the filling ingredients into the eggs, to make a thin custard.

HOMEMADE PUMPKIN FILLING
To make your own filling, roast large chunks of pumpkin with just a little oil for 30 minutes at 400°F, or until softened, or microwave them. Purée or mash well, then pass through a sieve until smooth. Add the rest of the ingredients once cooled.

7

Now we need to seal the pastry, as the filling is so liquid. Brush the pie shell all over with 1 tablespoon reserved beaten egg, then bake for 2 more minutes, until shiny.

8

Pull the oven rack out a little. Pour the filling into the crust, without letting it overflow, and slide the oven rack back in.

9

Bake for 45 minutes, or until the edges of the filling have risen slightly and the center wobbles gently. Let cool in the pan. To make the cream, whip the ingredients together until just thickened.

10

Serve the pie at room temperature or chilled, with the cream.

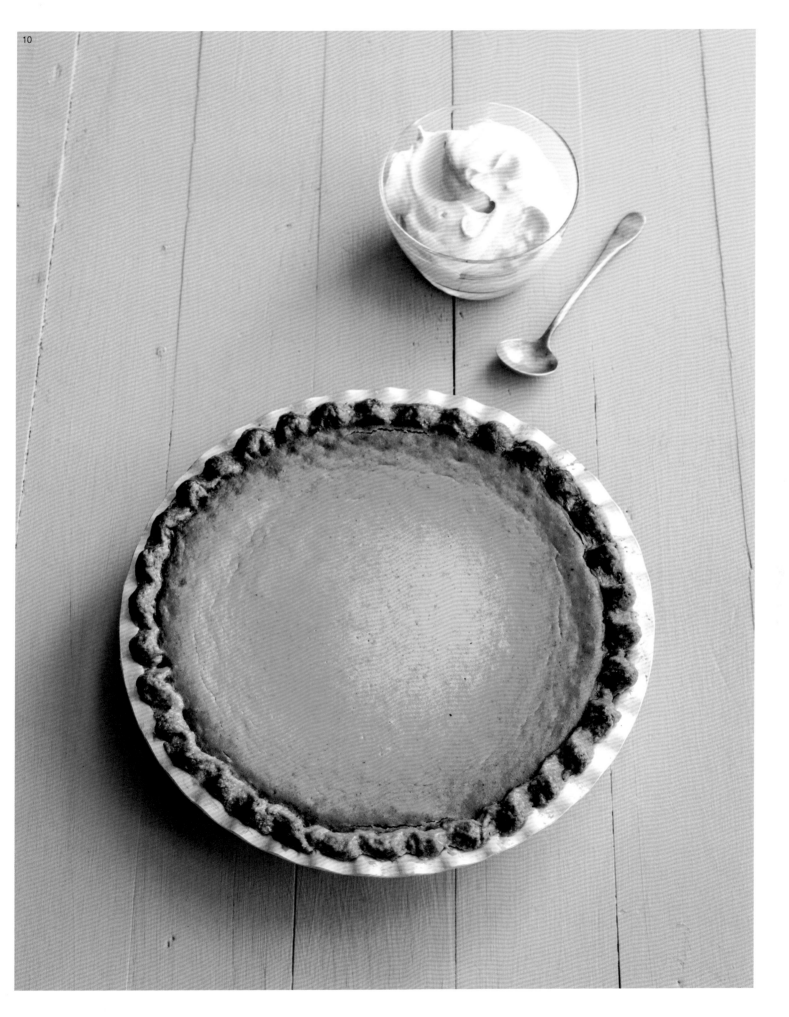

Angel Cake with Berries

Preparation time: 30 minutes,
plus cooling
Baking time: 35 minutes
Makes at least 12 slices

Angel food cake is like no other:
a soft, cloud-like sponge made
without yolks or fat, and not as
tricky as you might think. I like
serving it for dessert with a light,
creamy topping and seasonal fruit to
balance the sweetness, but you can
also use the cake recipe as a base
and get creative with one of the
other frostings in the book.

For the cake

1 vanilla bean or 1 tsp vanilla paste

1 orange

1 cup all-purpose flour, minus 1 tbsp

1 tbsp cornstarch

½ cup confectioners' sugar

½ tsp salt

10 eggs (whites only), at room
   temperature

1 tsp cream of tartar

1½ cups superfine sugar

For the topping

⅔ cup thick Greek yogurt

1 cup heavy cream

3–4 tbsp confectioners' sugar,
   or to taste

fresh summer berries and cherries,
   plus raspberry coulis, if you like
   (see page 154)

1
Preheat the oven to 350°F. Split the vanilla bean lengthwise and scrape out the seeds with the tip of the knife. Grate the zest from the orange, reserving the fruit for later. Mix the flour, cornstarch, confectioners' sugar, and salt, then sift together twice to make sure they are completely evenly mixed and lump-free.

2
Separate the eggs (see page 127), then put the whites in a large, scrupulously clean bowl with the cream of tartar. Using an electric mixer, whisk the whites until frothy and light. You won't need the yolks, but you could use them to make the lemon curd recipe on page 192.

WHICH BOWL FOR WHISKING?
A metal or ceramic bowl is best for whipping meringue mixtures— plastic bowls can hide little bits of grease in scratches, and grease is the enemy of fluffy egg whites.

3
Add the vanilla seeds and orange zest and keep whisking until the mixture holds itself in stiff peaks. The key is to stop beating before the meringue starts to look dry or separated at the edges.

4
Add 1 tablespoon of the superfine sugar, then beat again until the mixture returns to stiff peaks. Repeat this until all the sugar has been incorporated, and the meringue is thick and shimmery, like shaving cream.

5
Sift the flour mixture over the meringue. Using a large metal spoon, fold it in until combined and smooth, cutting and lifting the flour through the foam rather than stirring, to preserve the air bubbles.

6

Using a spatula, scrape the batter into a 10-inch angel food cake pan and level the top. The pan isn't greased or lined, as the cake needs to be able to "grip" and rise up the sides of the pan as it bakes.

7

Bake for 35 minutes, or until the cake is golden and has risen well. It's ready when a skewer inserted into the center comes out clean. Angel cakes need to be cooled upside-down. If your pan has feet, turn it over and let cool. If not, turn it upside down on a cooling rack or invert it onto a bottle, or something that will keep the top of the cake exposed to the air as it cools. Don't worry, it won't fall out. When the cake has cooled, carefully sweep an icing spatula around the pan to loosen it, then push the base of the pan up to expose the cake. You may need to ease the center of the pan away from the cake too.

8

Transfer the cake to a serving plate. To make the topping, squeeze 2 tablespoons juice from the orange and combine it with the yogurt, cream, and confectioners' sugar. Beat until smooth and thick. Taste and add more sugar, if you like. When ready to serve, smooth the topping over the cake either in a thick layer on top, or a thinner layer all over.

9

Serve with the berries and a little coulis, if you like.

TO MAKE YOUR OWN COULIS
Process or mash 4 cups fresh or frozen raspberries with 2 tablespoons confectioners' sugar until as smooth as possible, then strain out the pips. Taste and add more sugar if needed.

Sticky Pear & Pecan Toffee Cake

Preparation time: 20 minutes
Baking time: 50 minutes
Cuts into 12 slices

Many bakers have dreams of opening a little café with cakes on the counter and really good coffee. In mine, I'd be making this every day in fall, using plums, apples, or cranberries closer to the holidays. It's here in this chapter because I can imagine it crowning the table at Thanksgiving or Christmas.

For the cake

1 cup pitted soft dates

2 sticks (1 cup) soft butter, plus extra for greasing

1½ cups pecans

2 medium pears, just ripe (you need about 1½ cups chopped pear)

1 packed cup light brown sugar

4 eggs, room temperature

¼ cup milk

2⅓ cups all-purpose flour

1 tsp baking soda

1 tsp baking powder

2 tsp ground cinnamon or pumpkin pie spice

¼ tsp salt

For the toffee topping

½ packed cup light brown sugar

2 tbsp butter

⅓ cup heavy cream

½ cup pecans

1
First, soak the dates by covering them with boiling water. Let stand for 15 minutes, or longer if you like. Meanwhile, preheat the oven to 325°F and do the rest of the prep. Melt a little butter, then use a pastry brush to grease the inside of a 10-cup nonstick bundt pan.

NO BUNDT PAN?
Using a bundt pan gives this cake a wonderful texture and dramatic shape, but a greased and lined 9 x 13-inch sheet cake pan does the job too. Bake the cake at 325°F for 40 minutes, or until it has risen right to the middle, and a skewer inserted into the center comes out clean.

2
Finely chop the pecans in a food processor, then pour them out. Peel the pears, then cut them into fingertip-size chunks, discarding the central core part.

3
Drain the dates through a sieve. Process the butter and sugar together until creamy and smooth, then whizz in the dates. Now add the eggs, milk, flour, baking soda, baking powder, cinnamon, and salt and process to make a smooth cake batter.

MAKING IT BY HAND
This recipe is much easier with a food processor, but you can make it by hand too. Finely chop the nuts, and chop the soaked dates as finely as you can, almost to a pulp. Mix the dates and other ingredients in a large bowl and beat until creamy and smooth. Fold in the nuts and pears and continue as below.

4

Unless you have a really big food processor, at this point you'll need to turn the batter into a bowl to fold in the pecans and pears. If you do have the room in the processor bowl, be sure to remove the blades before mixing. Spoon the batter into the prepared pan and smooth the top.

5

Bake for 50 minutes, or until the cake has risen all over and a skewer inserted into the center comes out clean. Let the cake cool in the pan for at least 10 minutes before giving the pan a sharp tap on the work surface, then turning it out onto a cooling rack if serving cold, or a plate if serving warm.

6

For the toffee topping, put the sugar, butter, and cream in a medium pan. Heat it gently until the sugar has dissolved, then simmer briefly to make a silky smooth caramel sauce.

7

Stir the pecans into the sauce, then spoon it all over the cake. It will set firm and lose its shine if serving cold, but it will be easier to slice.

8

The cake will keep in an airtight container for up to 3 days, and will freeze well, without the topping.

TRY THIS
Make a double quantity of the sauce, and serve the sauce and the cake warm, at the table, as a spectacular dessert. Great with cream or crème anglaise served alongside.

Frosted Cupcakes

Preparation time: 25 minutes
plus cooling
Baking time: 18–20 minutes
Makes 12 cupcakes

When I teach baking, the thing most students seem to want to master is a good piped cupcake. It does take practice, but you'll soon be swirling frosting like a pro. Here, the classic recipe gets an upgrade with a white chocolate frosting that is easy to flavor, color, and pipe. Too fancy? Use the regular buttercream on page 46 and double it.

For the cupcakes

1½ sticks (¾ cup) butter

½ cup plus 2 tbsp buttermilk

4 eggs

1 tsp vanilla paste or extract

1 cup plus 3 tbsp all-purpose flour

2 tsp baking powder

¼ tsp salt

¾ cup plus 2 tbsp sugar, preferably superfine

1 cup almond meal

For the white chocolate frosting

½ cup heavy cream

3½ oz white chocolate

1½ sticks (¾ cup) soft butter

½ tsp vanilla paste or extract

a pinch of salt

2 cups confectioners' sugar

1

Line a 12-cup muffin pan with deep paper liners. Preheat the oven to 375°F. Melt the butter in a pan, remove from the heat, and let cool for a couple of minutes. Stir the buttermilk into the butter, then add the eggs and vanilla. Beat together with a fork until smooth.

2

Mix together the flour, baking powder, and salt, then sift into a large bowl. Stir in the sugar and almonds. Make a well in the center, then pour in the butter mixture.

3

Using a spatula or balloon whisk, quickly mix together until smooth and lump-free. Fill the liners using an ice cream scoop, or hold the bowl over the pan while you spoon it in. The liners should be quite full.

4

Bake for 18–20 minutes, or until they have risen evenly, are golden brown and smell sweet. Insert a skewer into one of the central cupcakes; it should come out clean. Let cool for 5 minutes, then transfer to a rack and cool completely.

5

To make the frosting, put the cream in a small pan and heat until the edges are just starting to bubble. Meanwhile, roughly chop the chocolate and put it in a small bowl. Pour the hot cream over the chocolate, then let it melt, stirring occasionally. Let cool completely.

6

Put the butter in a large bowl, beat well until creamy, add the vanilla and salt, then gradually beat in the confectioners' sugar until fluffy and pale. Gradually pour in the cooled chocolate, then beat to make a very light, smooth frosting. Work in more sugar if it seems too soft.

7

To frost with an icing spatula, mound 2 tablespoons frosting onto the cake. For neatly sloped sides, turn the cupcake clockwise in one hand while smoothing counter-clockwise with the other, holding the blade at a slight angle. Dip the knife into the frosting on top, turning it as before, to make an indent with a tall ridge around it. Clean the knife against the edge of the bowl before each stage.

8

To pipe roses, cut the first inch or so from a disposable pastry bag, insert a 2D rose tip, then spoon in the frosting. Don't fill it more than half full. Twist the pastry bag at the top to create pressure behind the tip. Start in the middle of the cake, then pipe outwards in a spiral. Pipe as evenly as you can, keeping the bag upright. If you mess up, scrape the frosting back into the bowl (avoiding crumbs) and try again. Twist the top of the bag to increase the pressure before piping each cake.

CHOCOLATE OREO CUPCAKES
Use 1 cup flour and 3 tablespoons cocoa powder in the batter. Use semi-sweet chocolate for the ganache, or crush some Oreos into the white frosting. Top with half a cookie.

PEANUT BUTTER CUPCAKES
Replace 3 tablespoons butter with smooth peanut butter in the basic batter. For the frosting, replace the chocolate and cream with ¾ cup smooth peanut butter. Top with Reese's Pieces.

PISTACHIO CUPCAKES
Grind 1½ cups shelled pistachios in a processor and add 1 cup to the batter instead of the almonds. Color the frosting with green food coloring. Frost the cakes, then sprinkle with the rest of the pistachios.

Red Velvet Whoopie Pies

Preparation time: 20 minutes,
plus cooling
Baking time: 10 minutes per batch
Makes 24 complete pies

If you feel like a change from cupcakes, whoopie pies are the answer. These attention-grabbing cakes are fun to make for Halloween or Valentine's. Unlike a classic whoopie, these are soft and delicate, like their namesake red velvet cake. Leave out the food coloring if you prefer, for a pale, chocolatey look.

For the batter

1½ sticks (¾ cup) soft butter,
    plus extra for greasing
1 cup superfine sugar
1 tsp vanilla bean paste or extract
2 cups all-purpose flour
¼ cup cocoa powder
1½ tsp baking soda
½ tsp baking powder
¼ tsp salt
3 eggs
½ cup buttermilk
1 tsp red food coloring paste

For the filling and decoration

1½ sticks (¾ cup) soft butter
14 oz full-fat cream cheese, cold
1¼ cups confectioners' sugar
1 tsp vanilla bean paste or extract
2 oz white chocolate

1

Preheat the oven to 350°F. Lightly grease and line 2 baking sheets with parchment paper. Put the butter, sugar, and vanilla in a large bowl and beat with an electric mixer or a wooden spoon until creamy and light.

2

Mix together the flour, cocoa, baking soda, baking powder, and salt, then sift them into a bowl. Put the eggs, buttermilk, and food coloring in the bowl with the butter and sugar.

3

Sift the flour mixture into the bowl, then beat to a smooth, bright-red batter. It will be fairly thick and sticky.

4

Spoon the mixture evenly onto the lined baking sheets, aiming for 48 balls, about 1 heaping teaspoon each. Leave room for the batter to spread a bit as it cooks. I use a small cookie scoop to get a nicely uniform round shape, but you can push the batter off the end of a spoon with your finger, or pipe it instead. You'll need to bake in several batches.

5

Bake the whoopies for 9–10 minutes, or until they have risen and are firm to the touch, but not crisp. Let cool for a few minutes on the sheets, then remove to a cooling rack and cool completely.

6

To make the filling, put the butter in a large bowl and beat with an electric mixer until very creamy and smooth. Add the cream cheese and vanilla and beat briefly until evenly blended. Now sift in the confectioners' sugar and beat for a few seconds more until smooth and creamy, or work it in gently with a spatula. If your kitchen is warm, chill the frosting while the whoopies cool.

7

Once cool, spread or pipe a generous amount of filling onto the flat sides of half the cakes, then top with the remaining halves and squeeze together gently so that the frosting shows at the sides.

8

Finely grate the white chocolate, then roll the edges of the whoopies in it to coat. It will stick to the filling.

9

Eat the whoopies the day they are made, or soon after. Keep them in the fridge, but eat them at room temperature. If you are not filling them immediately, pack them carefully with parchment paper between the layers.

BANOFFEE WHOOPIE PIES
Beat 1 mashed ripe banana into the creamed butter and sugar. Use 2 eggs and 2¼ cups flour and omit the cocoa. Sandwich with the filling plus 1 heaping teaspoon dulce de leche, then roll the edges in grated bittersweet chocolate.

PUMPKIN PIE WHOOPIE PIES
Use 1¼ cups light brown sugar. When creamed, beat in 1 cup canned pumpkin purée. Use 2 eggs, 2¼ cups flour (omitting the cocoa) and add 1 tablespoon pumpkin pie spice. Flavor the filling with the grated zest of 1 orange.

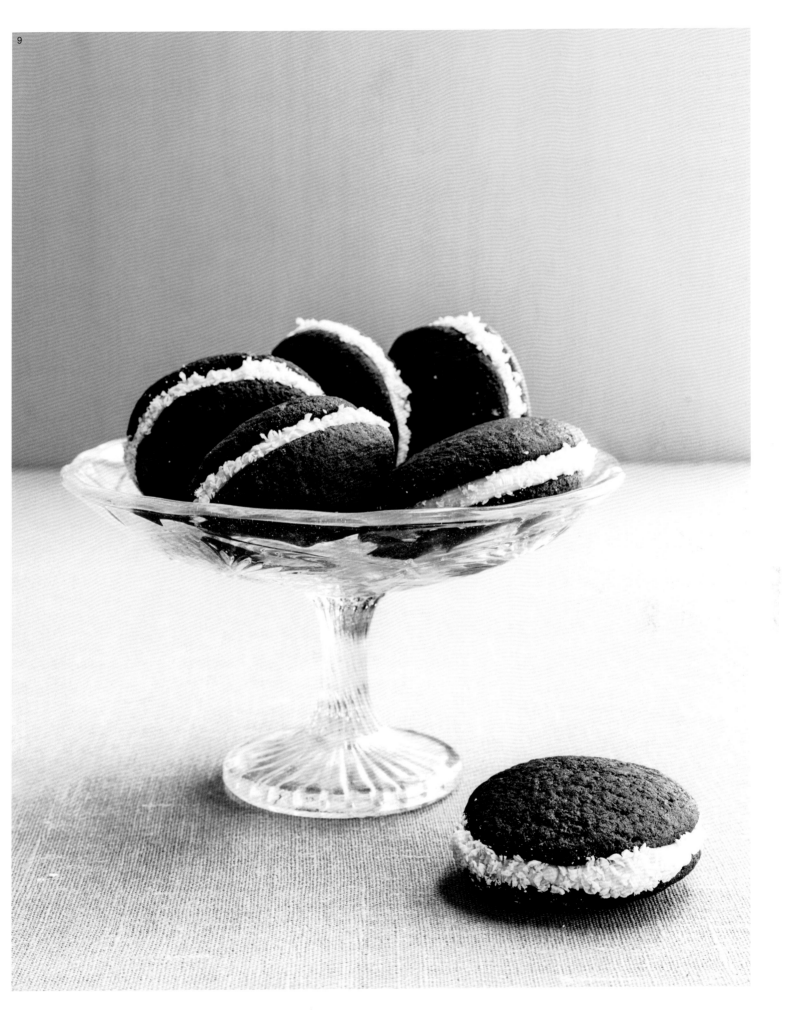

Vanilla Celebration Cake

Preparation time: about 1 hour
30–40 minutes, plus cooling
Baking time: 1 hour 40 minutes
Serves 20, or more (see page 10)

I'm often asked to make cakes
for weddings, anniversaries,
and birthdays, so I understand
the pressure you might feel if
you've been asked the same thing.
You need a reliable recipe that keeps
well, cuts cleanly, tastes good, and
looks fabulous. This recipe, a white
cake with extra eggs and a luxurious
white chocolate frosting, should do it.

For the cake

6 eggs, room temperature

3 sticks (1½ cups) soft butter,
 plus extra for greasing

1¾ cups sugar, ideally superfine

1 tsp vanilla bean paste

3 cups all-purpose flour

1 tbsp plus 1 tsp baking powder

¼ cup cornstarch

½ tsp salt

1¼ cups buttermilk

For the syrup

¼ cup sugar

½ tsp vanilla paste

For the frosting

1½ cups heavy cream

6 oz white chocolate

3 sticks (1½ cups) soft butter

1 tsp vanilla paste

¼ tsp salt

5½ cups confectioners' sugar,
 or more if needed

1
Preheat the oven to 325°F. Double-line a 9-inch springform or regular deep round cake pan (see page 177). Separate 3 of the eggs and add the whites to 3 whole eggs, ready for later. (You won't need the yolks here.)

2
Using an electric mixer, beat the butter, sugar, and vanilla together until very creamy and pale. Pour 1 egg white or egg into the bowl, then beat in until fluffy and light. Repeat until all the egg has been used. If the batter starts to look a little lumpy at any point, beat in 1 tablespoon of the flour.

3
Mix the flour, baking powder, cornstarch, and salt together in a bowl. Sift half of this into the cake batter, fold it in, then fold in the buttermilk. Follow with the rest of the flour mixture to make a smooth and fairly thick batter.

4
Spoon the batter into the pan and level the top. Make a slight dip in the center, which will encourage the cake to rise without a dome.

5
Bake for 1 hour 30–40 minutes, or until it has risen well and is golden, and a skewer inserted into the center comes out clean. Check carefully, as the cake may sink or seem heavy if underdone. In the meantime, make the syrup: gently heat the sugar, 3 tablespoons water, and vanilla until the sugar dissolves. Set aside. Once out of the oven, let the cake cool in the pan until just warm, then poke 25 holes right through it. Slowly spoon the syrup over it, letting it soak in after each addition. Let cool completely in the pan. It can be wrapped and frozen for up to 1 month.

6

For the frosting, put the cream in a small pan and heat until the edges are just starting to bubble. Chop the chocolate into small pieces and put in a small bowl. Pour the hot cream over it, then let it melt, stirring now and again, until smooth and silky. Let cool completely.

7

Put the butter, vanilla, and salt in a large bowl, beat well until smooth and creamy, then slowly beat in the confectioners' sugar to make a fluffy buttercream. Gradually pour in the cooled white chocolate and beat to make a very pale, silky-smooth frosting. If it seems too soft, add a little more sugar.

8

Split the cake horizontally into 3 even layers using a large serrated knife (see page 136). Stack it back together, spreading 1 cup frosting between each layer.

9

Now we're going to cover the cake in a "crumb coat," which gives it a perfect finish. Mound 1¼ cups of the frosting onto the cake, then spread it over the top and down the sides to meet the plate. Try not to lift the icing spatula off the cake, but move it in a fluid movement. Smooth, then chill for 10 minutes, or until firm.

10

Spread the remaining frosting over the cake as before. If this all sounds too tricky, leave the frosting ruffled and rustic. Store in a cool place (or the fridge if it's a hot day) to let the frosting set a little. It can be wrapped and chilled for up to 2 days; allow to come to room temperature before eating. To top with flowers, tie together your favorite blooms, wrap the ends in plastic wrap, then sit them on top of or to the side of the cake.

Chocolate Hazelnut Log

Preparation time: 35 minutes,
plus chilling
Baking time: 15 minutes
Serves 8–10

This variation on a classic Yule log
is a perfect Christmas treat that kids
will love to help with. But don't just
save it for December; when scored
and rolled from one of the narrow
ends, it makes a fat, swirly roulade
for a special dessert at any time of
year. Use 70% bittersweet chocolate
and serve it with berries.

For the cake

a little butter, for greasing

6 eggs, room temperature

¾ packed cup light brown sugar

1 tbsp all-purpose flour

a pinch of salt

½ cup good-quality cocoa powder,
   plus 2 tbsp for rolling

For the filling

7 oz bittersweet chocolate,
   60% cocoa solids

2½ cups heavy cream

7 oz (¾ cup) Nutella

1 tsp vanilla extract

confectioners' sugar, to dust

1
Grease the base and sides of a 10 x 15-inch jelly roll pan or rimmed baking sheet, then line the base with parchment paper. Preheat the oven to 350°F. Put the eggs and the sugar in a large bowl and whisk with an electric mixer at medium speed until thick, mousse-like, and doubled in volume. It will take 5 minutes or so.

2
Mix the flour, salt, and cocoa in a bowl, then sift them over the whisked eggs. Fold them in using a large metal spoon or spatula, cutting and lifting rather than stirring. This will preserve the air bubbles trapped inside the batter. It might take longer than you expect to get the batter to an almost even brown.

3
Holding the bowl just above the prepared baking pan (pouring from a great height will knock the bubbles flat), pour in the cake batter. Tilt the pan slowly from side to side, letting the batter run into the corners.

4
Bake for 15 minutes, or until the cake has risen all over and the sides are shrinking away from the edge of the pan. It's best to loosen the cake away from the pan carefully with an icing spatula now, in case it has stuck a little.

5
Spread a large sheet of parchment paper on the work surface, then sift the 2 tablespoons cocoa powder over it. Flip the cake onto this sheet, remove the pan, then cover the cake with a clean dish towel and let cool. The cloth will trap moisture as the cake cools, helping it stay soft and moist.

6

Make the filling. Chop the chocolate into small pieces. Heat 1¼ cups of the cream in a pan until it bubbles at the edges. Take off the heat and stir in the chocolate, Nutella, and vanilla. Let it melt until smooth, then set aside until it has cooled, but is still fairly liquid.

7

Pour the rest of the cream into a bowl, add about ½ cup of the chocolate ganache, then whisk until very thick, but not stiff.

8

When the cake has cooled, remove the dish towel, then carefully peel off the parchment paper. Trim about ½ inch off each edge with a serrated knife. Score a line in the cake about 1 inch in from the nearest long end.

9

Spread the filling over the cake, then roll it up from the scored end. Use the paper to help make a tight roll.

10

Roll the cake onto a clean piece of parchment. Cut about 4 inches off one end, at an angle.

11

Transfer the large piece to a serving plate, then nestle the shorter one against it to make a branch. Spread the remaining ganache all over, adding plenty of texture with the knife. Chill for at least 1 hour or up to 3 days.

12

Remove from the fridge 30 minutes before eating and dust with confectioners' sugar to serve.

Festive Fruit Cake

Preparation time: 30 minutes, plus
soaking and optional feeding time
Baking time: 2¾–3 hours
Makes about 24 slices

A classic rich fruit cake is a
traditional British recipe that's well
worth trying for yourself—it's a lot
more satisfying than buying ready-
made. It can be eaten immediately,
or matured and fed with alcohol.
Use whatever dried fruit you like,
and the decorating is optional—see
the tips on page 177 and 180.

For the cake

1 lemon

⅔ cup glacé cherries, drained

4¼ cups dried mixed fruit, such as
   raisins, sultanas, or currants

⅔ cup candied mixed citrus peel

½ cup brandy or dark rum (see Tip)

2 sticks (1 cup) soft butter, plus
   extra for greasing

1 packed cup plus 2 tbsp light
   brown sugar

1 tsp vanilla extract

4 eggs

1¾ cups all-purpose flour

2 tsp pumpkin pie spice

¼ tsp salt

½ cup toasted sliced almonds

To decorate

2 tbsp apricot jam, marmalade
   or cake glaze

1 lb 2 oz ready-made marzipan

1 lb 2 oz ready-to-roll fondant icing

confectioners' sugar, for dusting

ribbon and edible glitter (optional),
   or decorations of your choice

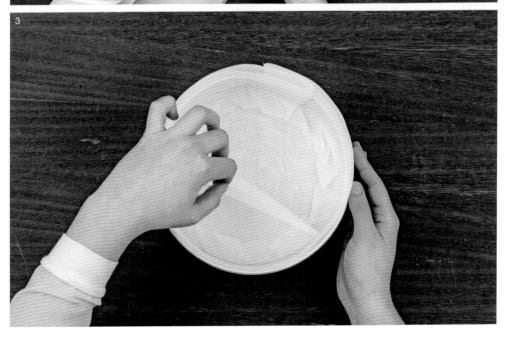

1

Finely grate the zest from the lemon and squeeze the juice. Cut the cherries in half. Put them into a large saucepan with the dried fruit and peel, and all but 2 tablespoons of the alcohol. Cover, then bring to a simmer. Remove from the heat and let stand for at least 1 hour, or overnight if you can. The fruit will plump up and absorb the liquid.

SOAKING ALTERNATIVES
If you'd rather not use alcohol, strong black tea makes a good substitute, as does orange or apple juice. Alcohol is added to act as a flavoring, as well as to preserve the cake until the holidays. Any dried fruit can be substituted, although I'd recommend a balance of sweet and tart fruit for a more interesting end result. If you can't find glacé cherries, use maraschino.

2

When ready to make the cake, preheat the oven to 325°F. Double-line a deep, 8-inch round cake pan with parchment paper. To do this, fold a 26 x 12-inch piece of parchment in half lengthwise. On the folded side, make a fold about ¾ inch of the way in. Snip at ¾-inch intervals along the length of the seam, up to the fold, to make a frill. Cut 2 circles for the base.

3

Grease the pan with butter, then line the sides with the frilled paper, with the frills at the base of the pan, overlapping slightly. Grease the circles with butter, then sit them on top, trapping the frill below. This preparation is needed to protect the cake during the long baking time.

4

Put the butter and sugar in a large bowl, then beat with an electric mixer until pale and creamy. Add the vanilla, then beat in 1 egg. When the mixture is fluffy and light, add the next egg and repeat. If the batter starts to look a little lumpy, beat in 1 tablespoon of the flour. Repeat with the remaining eggs.

5

Sift the flour, spice, and salt into the bowl and fold into the batter with a spatula or large metal spoon. Now fold in the soaked fruit, plus the nuts. It will make a stiff batter.

6

Scrape the batter into the prepared pan and level the top. Make a depression in the middle of the batter with the spatula. This will help the cake rise more evenly.

7
Bake for 1½ hours, then turn the oven down to 300°F for 1¼–1½ hours more. When ready, the cake will be dark golden, and a skewer inserted into the center will come out clean. If not, bake for another 15 minutes and check again. Let cool in its pan on a rack. When still warm, prick holes all over it with a toothpick and spoon in the rest of the alcohol, tea or juice. Once cool, remove from the pan, then wrap carefully in clean parchment paper and store in an airtight container in a cool place.

FEEDING YOUR CAKE
This cake is perfectly good when eaten as soon as it's cooled, but it can be matured over a couple of months. Spoon 1 tablespoon of your chosen soaking liquid over it 3 times before Christmas, allowing at least 1 week between each feeding. Wrap and store carefully each time to prevent the cake from drying out.

8
When ready to decorate, choose a cake plate or board that's a little larger than the cake itself. Melt the jam, marmalade, or cake glaze with 1 teaspoon water, then push it through a sieve to remove any lumps. Brush the strained jam over the top of the cake. This will be the glue for the marzipan.

9
Dust the work surface generously with confectioners' sugar. Knead the marzipan a few times to soften it a little, then shape it into a ball. Roll with a rolling pin, turning the marzipan by 90 degrees with every few rolls, until it is a circle about the same size as the cake. Use your hands to help shape the circle if it's a little uneven. Put it on the cake.

ICING ALTERNATIVES

Half-covering the cake is a great way to try your hand at icing without the challenge of covering a cake entirely. Or, if you'd rather avoid cake decorating all together, why not press whole shelled almonds into the top of the cake instead, before baking? When ready to serve, brush with the glaze or dust with confectioners' sugar and fix a ribbon around it.

10

Making sure there are no lumps of marzipan on the work surface, repeat the process using two thirds of the fondant icing, shaping it with your hands if you need to. Roll the rest of the icing to about ⅛ inch thick, then cut out festive shapes with a cookie cutter.

11

Bring some water to a boil and let it cool a little. Dampen a clean pastry brush in the boiled water and, sparingly but evenly, brush it over the marzipan. Lay the fondant on top of the marzipan, then stick the cut-out shapes on top, again using a little water as glue. Sprinkle with edible glitter (if using) and tie a ribbon around the cake.

12

Let the fondant dry for a few hours, then store in an airtight container until needed.

NOT QUITE STRAIGHT?

If the circle of marzipan or fondant is too big once it's on the cake, don't worry. If it's too big, gently rub a tall, straight-sided glass around the edge of the cake, which will press the fondant and marzipan in and level things up. If the circle is too small, rub it with the flat of your hand to press it outwards a little.

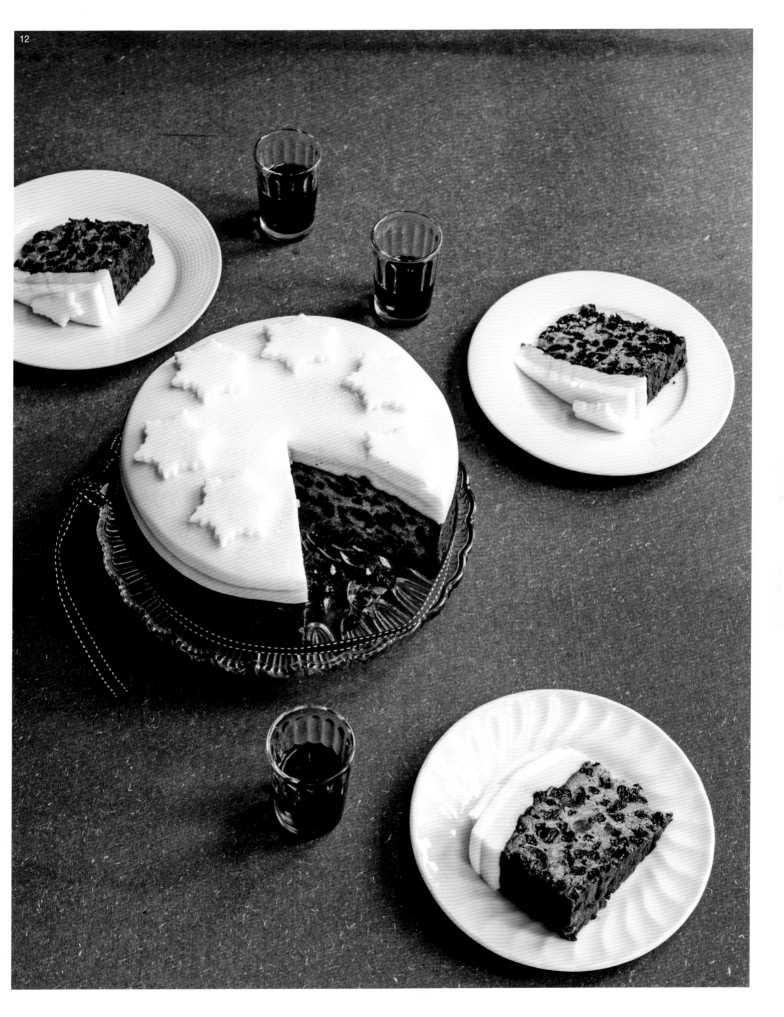

Cranberry Stollen

Preparation time: 45 minutes,
plus rising, proofing, and cooling
Baking time: 30 minutes
Makes 2 family-size loaves

Several wintry trips to Germany have
given me a real fondness for stollen,
the richly fruited Christmas loaf
with the hidden treasure of marzipan
inside. The recipe makes two loaves;
eat one straight after baking, then
wrap the other one well and stash it
in the freezer for up to 1 month.

___

For the bread

1 lemon

¼ cup rum (or use orange juice)

1 tsp vanilla extract

1 cup dried cranberries

1 cup golden raisins (or use
   chopped dried apricots)

1¼ cups milk

1 tbsp instant dry yeast

1 whole nutmeg, or use 1 tsp ground

4 cups bread flour, plus extra
   for kneading

1 tsp salt

⅓ cup sugar

1½ sticks (¾ cup) butter

2 eggs

9 oz marzipan

To finish

½ stick (¼ cup) butter

¼ cup confectioners' sugar

1

Finely grate the lemon zest and mix it with the rum or orange juice, vanilla, and dried fruit. Let macerate while you make the dough. Gently warm the milk in the microwave or in a pan, then whisk in the yeast. The milk must only be warm; if it's too hot, it will kill the yeast.

2

If using whole nutmeg, grate 2 teaspoons. Sift the flour into a large bowl with the salt, then add the nutmeg and sugar. Cut the butter into cubes, then rub it into the flour mixture using your fingertips, until the mixture looks like breadcrumbs.

3

Separate one of the eggs (see page 127). Add the yolk and whole egg to the milk and beat together. Using a wooden spoon, mix the liquid into the rubbed-in mixture to make a soft, sticky dough. Let stand for 10 minutes.

4

Dust the work surface with flour, then turn the dough out onto it. Flour the top of the dough and your hands, then begin to knead (see page 69 for guidance). Keep going for about 10 minutes, until the dough feels very springy or elastic and silky smooth. Use more flour if you need to. Put the dough in an oiled bowl and cover with oiled plastic wrap.

5

Let rise in a warm place for about 1½ hours, or until doubled in size.

6

Turn the dough out onto the floured work surface and cut it in half. Use your hands to press and pat each half into a rectangle about 8 x 15 inches. Spread the soaked fruit over the bottom half of each rectangle, then fold the top half over it.

7

Pat the dough out to about 6 x 10 inches, then fold it in half again along the long edge; repeat this twice, or until the fruit is well distributed in the dough, but isn't escaping. You should end up with 2 rectangles about 6 x 10 inches. If at any point it starts being too springy to handle, let it sit for a few minutes, then continue.

8

Roll the marzipan into 2 equal sausages. Make a deep groove along the length of each piece of dough, then place the marzipan in it.

9

Roll the left side of the dough over the marzipan. Press and pinch the edges together well to make a lip of dough, then shape the ends of the loaves into slight points.

10

Line a large baking sheet with parchment paper and lift the breads onto it. Leave room for rising. Cover with oiled plastic wrap and let proof in a warm place for 1 hour, or until almost doubled in size. Preheat the oven to 350°F.

11

Bake for 30 minutes, or until the breads have risen well and are dark golden brown. Melt the butter, then brush it all over the warm stollen and dredge with confectioners' sugar.

12

Let cool completely before wrapping and storing. Dust with sugar again before bringing it to the table.

DESSERTS

&

AFTER DINNER

Flourless Chocolate Cake

Preparation time: 20 minutes
Baking time: 35 minutes
Serves 12

A flourless chocolate cake is
my dessert hero, especially when
feeding friends who are avoiding
wheat. Luckily, this kind of cake is
best made without flour anyway,
the nuts and chocolate providing
the structure and a decadently gooey
texture within. The espresso bolsters
the chocolate flavor rather than
adding a coffee taste of its own.

1¾ sticks (¾ cup plus 2 tbsp)
  butter, plus extra for greasing

1 cup skinned hazelnuts (or almond
  meal, see Tip)

1 packed cup light brown sugar

7 oz bittersweet chocolate,
  70% cocoa solids

2 tbsp fresh espresso or 1 tbsp
  instant espresso mixed
  with 2 tbsp just-boiled water

1 tsp vanilla extract

5 eggs, room temperature

¼ tsp salt

1 tbsp cocoa powder, for dusting

1

Generously grease a 9-inch round springform pan with butter, then line the base with parchment paper. Preheat the oven to 350°F. Put the nuts in a food processor with 1 tablespoon of the sugar, then process until finely ground. If using almond meal, skip this step and add the sugar later on.

NUT OPTIONS
If you can't find pre-skinned (sometimes labeled as blanched) hazelnuts, buy skin-on instead and remove the skins at home. Spread them out in a roasting pan and cook for 8–10 minutes at 350°F until the skins start to crack and look flaky. Pour them into a clean dish towel and rub vigorously to loosen. If a few skins remain attached, don't worry. Let them cool before grinding them. This process will also toast the nuts, giving a rounded and full flavor to your cake. Or, to make the whole process quicker, you could use 1¼ cups almond meal instead.

2

Break the chocolate into a medium heatproof bowl and add the butter, coffee, and vanilla. Melt together gently, either set over a pan of barely simmering water, or in the microwave. Stir until smooth, then set aside.

3

Crack the eggs into a large bowl, add the rest of the sugar, then whisk for 5 minutes with an electric mixer until thick, mousse-like, and doubled in volume.

4

Pour the melted chocolate around the edge of the bowl (this prevents it from knocking too much air out of the foam). Using a large metal spoon, fold the chocolate in. It might take longer than you expect to get the batter to an almost even brown, and before little ribbons of chocolate stop appearing.

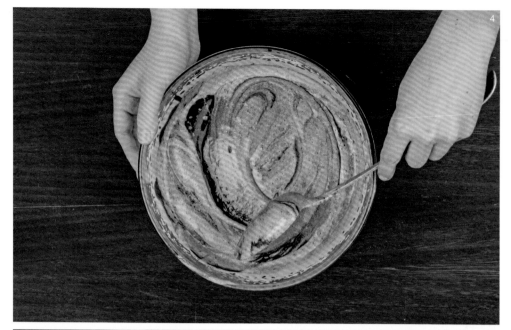

5

Sprinkle the ground nuts and salt into the bowl, then fold them in until evenly blended. Carefully pour the batter into the prepared pan. Preserving the air is the name of the game.

6

Bake on the middle shelf of the oven for about 35 minutes, or until the cake has risen and is set on top, with a just-perceptible wobble underneath the papery crust when you jiggle the pan. Put the pan on a cooling rack as it cools. The torte will sink and crack a little, which is fine.

7

If serving the cake cold, it's easy to transfer it to a plate: just unclip the sides of the pan and use an icing spatula to loosen the cake and its lining paper away from the base. To serve warm, leave it in the pan, as the cake is quite delicate. Put the cocoa in a fine-mesh sieve and give the cake a good dusting. Serve with whipped cream, ice cream, and perhaps some berries if you like. The cake can be made up to 2 days ahead (I actually prefer it the next day) and kept in a cool place. Let it come to room temperature before serving.

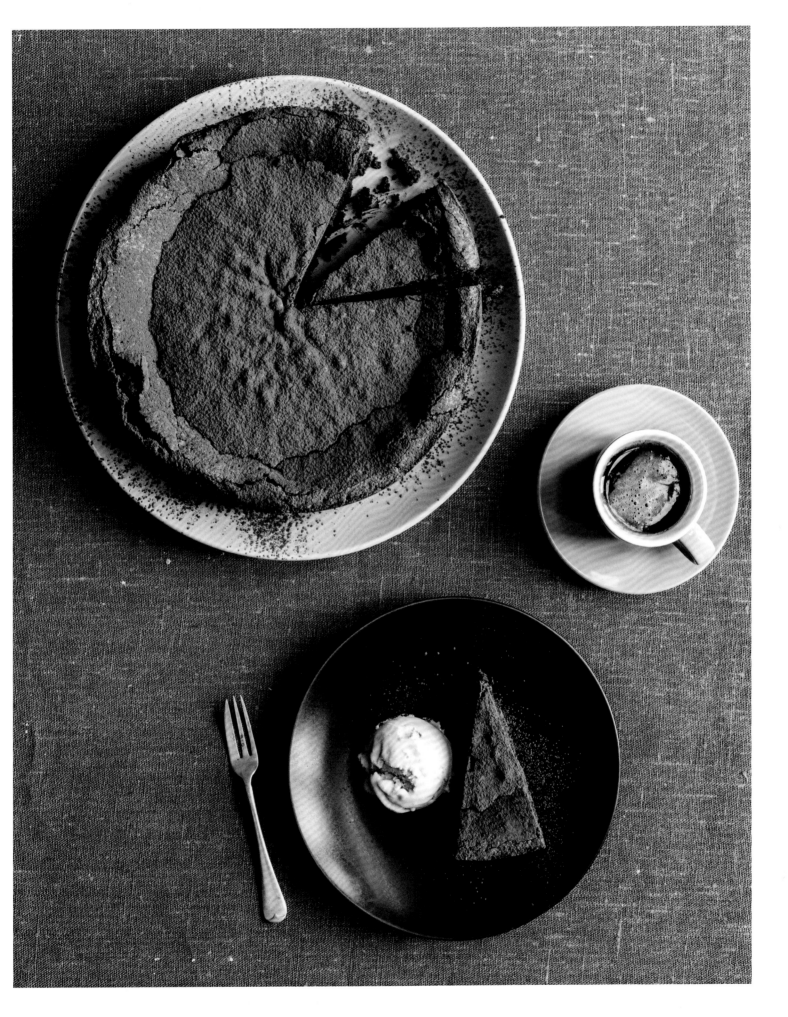

Tart au Citron

Preparation time: about 1 hour 10 minutes (including blind baking), plus chilling and cooling
Baking time: 5 minutes
Serves 12

I turn to classic lemon tart again and again for a dessert that works for just about any meal. The lemon curd filling is sharp, fresh, and citrussy, and the pastry is a crisp, sweet shell that's simple to make, with no need to worry about over-mixing. There's enough pastry for two tarts here, so put half in the freezer for next time.

For the pastry

1 egg

2 sticks (1 cup) soft butter

1 tsp vanilla extract

⅓ cup confectioners' sugar

½ tsp fine salt

2¾ cups all-purpose flour,
   plus extra for rolling

For the lemon curd filling

8 eggs

1½ sticks (¾ cup) butter

1 cup sugar

5 large lemons, juiced
   (you'll need 1 cup juice)

1
To make the pastry, first separate the egg (see page 127). You will only need the yolk. In a large bowl, beat the butter until it is very soft and smooth. Next, add the egg yolk, vanilla, sugar, and salt.

2
Beat together until evenly combined and creamy. Sift in the flour, then work it into the creamed mixture until you have a clumpy but evenly mixed dough, with hardly any dry flour left at the bottom of the bowl.

MAKE IT IN A PROCESSOR
It's very easy to make the pastry by hand, but if you have a food processor, then simply pulse the butter by itself until creamy, pulse in the yolk, vanilla, sugar, and salt, then finish with the flour.

3
Turn out the dough onto the work surface and squish it together to make a smooth ball. It will seem soft, even a bit sticky. Shape into 2 equal discs, then wrap in plastic wrap. Chill one piece for at least 30 minutes (you need it to be firm but not hard, or it will crack as it rolls), and reserve the other for another time. It can be frozen for up to 1 month.

4
Preheat the oven to 400°F and use the pastry to line a 9-inch fluted tart pan. Before rolling, flour the work surface and rolling pin. Press shallow ridges across the pastry, then rotate it by a quarter turn. Repeat this until the pastry is about ½ inch thick. If any cracks do appear, pinch them together.

5

Now roll out the pastry to a circle. Roll the pin evenly over the pastry, going forwards and backwards in one direction only. If you roll it in several directions, the pastry is likely to roll unevenly and stretch, which causes shrinking. Turn it by a quarter turn every few rolls, until it is just large enough to line the pan, allowing about a 1-inch overhang.

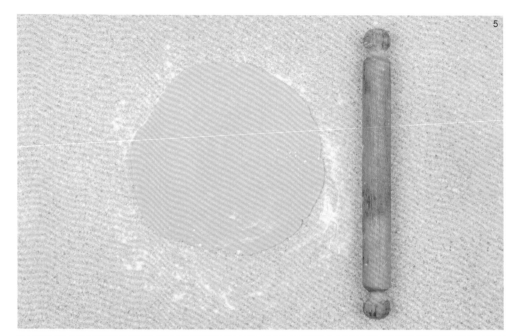

6

Flip the farthest edge of the pastry over the rolling pin, then lift it and carefully drape it over the pan. Taking it a section at a time, push it gently down and into the corner of the pan so it sits in a nice clean right angle. Now pinch off a small ball of excess pastry and use it to press the pastry into the ridges of the pan.

7

Trim the excess pastry away cleanly with a quick roll of the rolling pin across the top of the pan. Pinch the pastry between your finger and thumb so that its edge meets the top of the pan, or better still, comes slightly higher (that way, even if your pastry does shrink, it will still be the same size as the pan). Prick the base all over with a fork, going right down to the metal. Lift onto a baking sheet and chill for 10 minutes in the freezer until hard, or longer in the fridge if you have time.

ANY HOLES?

If any holes or tears appear, simply dampen a little piece of the leftover pastry dough and press it into the hole or tear. If cracks appear during baking, smooth a blob of pastry dough over the hot pastry, bake for a few minutes to set, and it will melt and form a delicate seal. Be careful when doing this, though, as too much pressure on the edge of a baked pastry shell can cause crumbling—this is for emergency measures only!

8

When ready to bake, line the pastry with a sheet of foil, making sure all the edges are covered. I tend not to use parchment for this, as it can make the pastry sweaty underneath. Fill with pie weights, mounding them up a little at the sides, to support the pastry as it bakes.

9

Bake for 15–20 minutes, or until the pastry looks set and is fairly dry underneath the foil. It should not have taken on much color at this point. Removing the beans too soon can cause the pastry to sag, so if you're not sure, give it another 5 minutes. Remove the foil and beans from the pan.

10

Turn the oven down to 325°F. Bake for another 10–15 minutes, or until the bottom of the pastry is pale gold and feels sandy. If the outside edges are looking brown before the middle of the pastry is ready, carefully wrap in foil and return to the oven.

11

While the pastry is baking, make the filling. Separate 4 eggs (see page 127). You will only need the yolks for this recipe. Beat them with the 4 whole eggs in a large bowl. Cut the butter into small pieces, and put in a heavy-based pan with the sugar and lemon juice.

12

Gently melt the butter and sugar into the lemon juice. Once melted, begin to whisk the eggs with one hand, and simultaneously pour the hot lemon mixture onto them with the other. Pour slowly at first so that the eggs don't get too hot too quickly, and scramble.

13

Return the mixture to the pan and cook it over medium heat for 3–5 minutes, or until thickened and smooth. Try to avoid letting it boil, and keep stirring all the time, concentrating on the edges of the pan where it is hottest.

14

Pour the lemon curd into the cooked pastry shell, the bake again for 5 minutes, which just helps the curd to set.

15

Transfer the tart to a cooling rack, let cool completely, then chill until ready to serve. Dredge with confectioners' sugar, if you like.

LEMON MERINGUE PIE
To transform the tart into a lemon meringue pie, follow the meringue technique on page 199, beating 4 of the leftover egg whites with 1 cup superfine sugar. Whisk 1 teaspoon cornstarch into the thick finished meringue. Dollop evenly over the warm lemon filling, then spread it up to and slightly over the pastry edges, peaking the meringue in dramatic curls as you go. Bake at 400°F for 20 minutes or until golden, let cool for at least 1 hour, then serve warm or cold on the day of making.

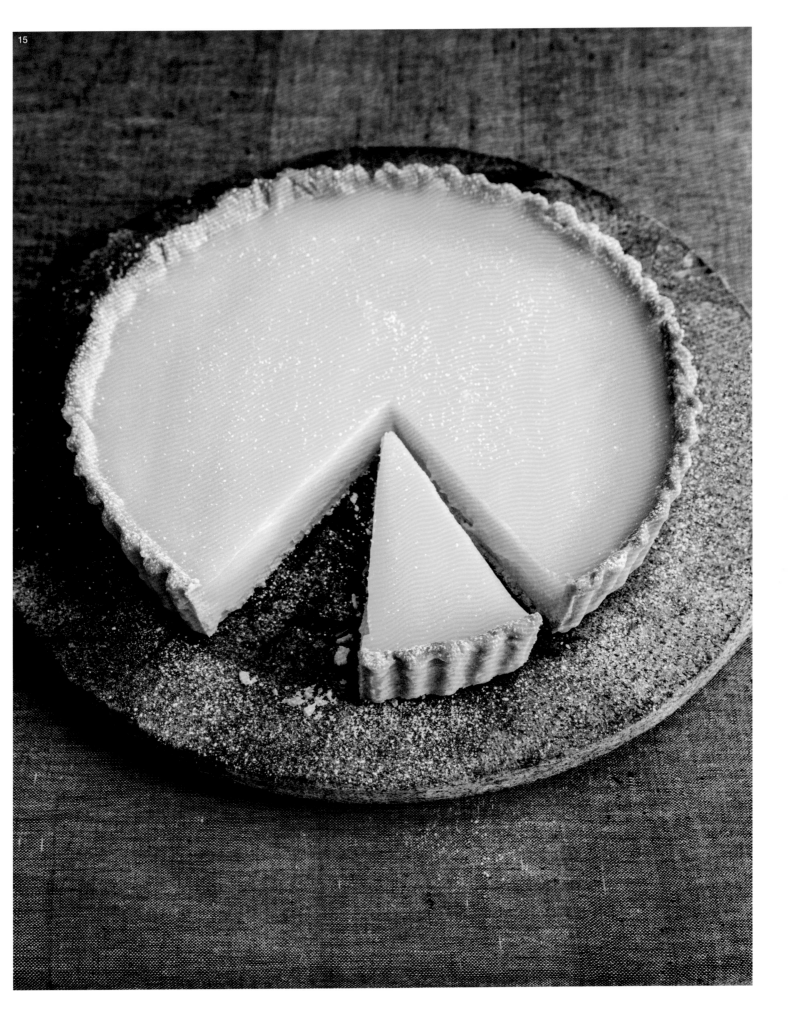

Strawberry Meringue Cake

Preparation time: 30 minutes
Baking time: about 1 hour
Serves 12

Crisp and fruity, soft and cakey, this playful bake is inspired by that British classic, Eton mess, and makes a great alternative to a pavlova for an unusual summer dessert. Just like Eton mess, the cream is absolutely key to the finished recipe. Pour it lavishly over each portion so it soaks into the cake and mingles with the berries and meringue.

For the cake

1 stick (½ cup) butter, plus extra
    for greasing
¼ cup heavy or whipping cream,
    plus extra to serve
1 tsp vanilla paste, or use extract
9 oz ripe strawberries
1⅓ cups all-purpose flour
1 cup almond meal
½ tsp baking powder
¼ tsp salt
3 eggs plus 2 yolks
¾ cup superfine sugar

For the topping

2 egg whites
½ cup superfine sugar
more ripe strawberries,
    or other summer fruit
1 tbsp confectioners' sugar

1
Preheat the oven to 350°F. Use a little butter to grease a 9-inch round springform cake pan, then line the base with parchment. Separate 2 eggs (see page 127), putting the yolks in a large bowl to use in the cake batter later, and the whites in another large bowl for the meringue.

2
Get the meringue ready first. Using an electric mixer, whisk the egg whites until the beaters leave a stiff peak when you pull them away from the bowl. Be careful not to overwhisk them.

3
Add 1 tablespoon of the sugar, then beat until the mixture becomes thick, shiny, and holds stiff peaks. Keep adding and whisking back to stiff peaks until all the sugar has been used and the meringue has taken on a pearly sheen.

TOO MUCH EFFORT?
If you like the idea of this cake, but want to reduce the number of steps, simply poke a good handful of crushed ready-made meringue shells into the cake batter before baking.

4
Now for the cake. Melt the butter in a small pan, then remove from the heat and stir in the cream and vanilla. Remove the stems from the strawberries, then cut into fingertip-size chunks. You should have about 1¾ cups prepared fruit.

5
Mix the flour, almond meal, baking powder, and salt and set aside for later. Crack the 3 whole eggs into the bowl containing the 2 yolks from earlier, then add the superfine sugar.

6

Using the electric mixer, beat the eggs and sugar together until doubled in volume, thick and mousse-like, which will take about 5 minutes.

7

Pour the butter mixture into the eggs, whisk briefly, then sift the flour and almond mixture over the top. Whisk briefly again, until evenly blended. Fold in the chopped strawberries, using a large spoon or spatula.

8

Pour the batter into the prepared pan and level the top. Spoon the meringue over the cake to make a sort of crown, with nice pointy peaks if you can. Leave some of the middle of the cake uncovered, as it takes too long to bake otherwise. If the meringue has set a little in the bowl, just fold it a few times with the spoon until smooth.

9

Bake for 10 minutes, then turn the oven down to 325°F and bake for 45–50 minutes more, or until the cake is golden, has risen in the middle, and the meringue is crisp and feels dry and hard. Insert a skewer to see if it is ready. It will come out clean or just a little sticky when done. Let cool for a while in the pan, then carefully unclip it. Let cool on a rack, then remove the base and transfer to a serving plate once cooled.

10

Serve the cake with more strawberries on top and to the side, with a dusting of confectioners' sugar and a good splash of cream.

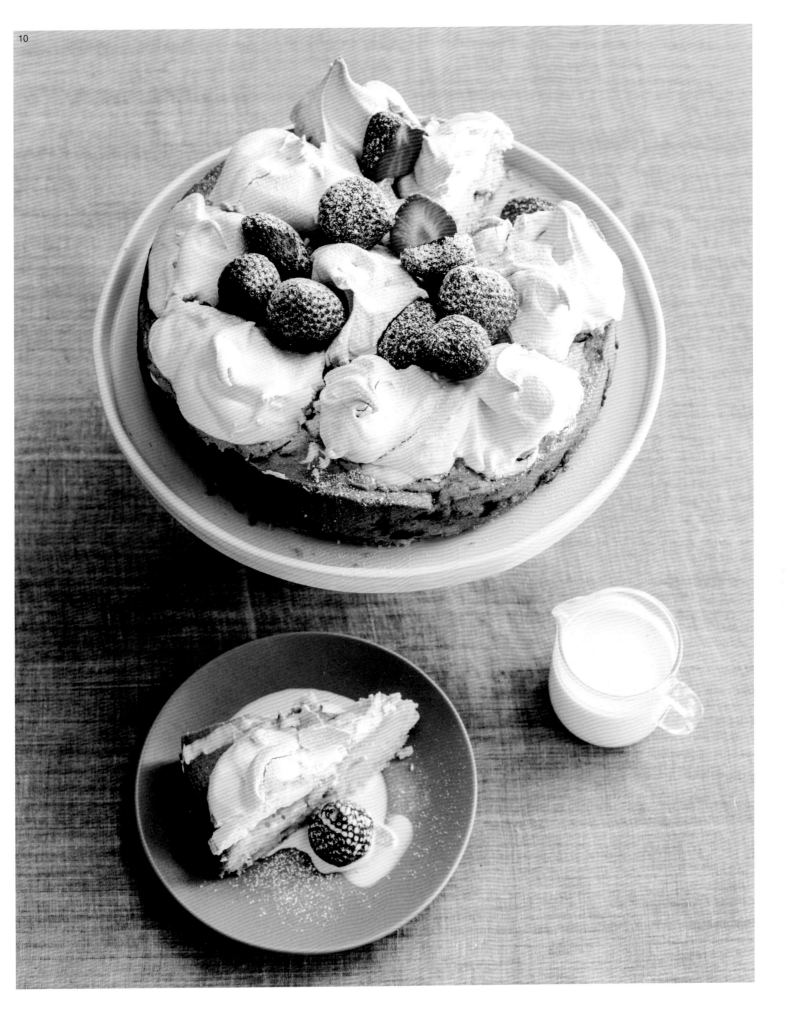

Whole Orange & Almond Cake

Preparation time: 10 minutes,
plus 2 hours for boiling the oranges
Baking time: 50 minutes
Serves 12

Whole oranges, skin and all, are
cooked until completely tender,
then blended with almonds, eggs,
and a little olive oil in this Spanish-
style, naturally gluten-free cake.
Its texture is light but rich, with a
marmaladey quality.

---

2 medium oranges,
    about 6½ oz each
2 tbsp extra-virgin olive oil,
    plus extra for greasing
1¼ cups sugar
6 eggs, room temperature
3 cups almond meal
1 tbsp baking powder
    (a gluten-free brand if needed)
¼ tsp salt
a handful of sliced almonds
thick Greek yogurt or crème fraîche,
    to serve (optional)

1

Put the oranges in a medium pan, then cover with water and a lid. Bring to a simmer, then boil for 2 hours, or until the oranges are very soft when you poke them with a knife. The oranges will bob around a bit, so check them after 1 hour and turn them over to make sure they cook evenly. Add more water while you're there, if needed.

ORANGES IN THE MICROWAVE
If you have a microwave, cut the oranges in half (whole ones will explode), put them in a microwave-proof bowl with a splash of water and cover with plastic wrap. Pierce a few holes in the wrap. Cook on full power for 10 minutes, or until completely tender (it may take longer, depending on your microwave). Let cool for a few minutes before removing the wrap.

2

Grease a 9-inch round springform pan with a little oil, then line with parchment paper. Preheat the oven to 350°F. Drain the oranges, and when cool enough to handle, cut into large pieces and remove any pips. Put them, skin and all, in a food processor. Add the sugar and pulse to a smooth purée.

3

Add the eggs to the processor, then whizz for about 1 minute until paler and thickened.

4

Pour in the almond meal, baking powder, salt, and oil and process for a few seconds to make a smooth, evenly blended batter. Using a spatula, scrape the batter into the prepared pan, smooth the top, then scatter with the sliced almonds.

5

Bake for 50 minutes, or until the cake is golden all over and has risen all the way to the center, and a skewer inserted in the middle comes out clean. Remove and let cool in the pan for 10 minutes (the cake will sink back down to become flat), then run an icing spatula between the cake and the pan and unclip the sides. Let the cake cool on the pan base, on a cooling rack.

6

There's a trick to getting a cake with a loose topping onto a plate without any dramas. Flip the cake upside down onto a flat plate, then remove the pan base and parchment paper. Put a serving plate on top, then turn it the right way up. Serve with thick Greek yogurt or crème fraîche.

Chocolate Profiteroles

Preparation time: 20 minutes,
plus cooling
Baking time: 30 minutes per batch
Serves 6 (makes 18)

Once you've discovered how
easy it is to make choux pastry at
home, you'll be making profiteroles
again and again. Cooled, unfilled
choux puffs will keep in an airtight
container for 3 days or freeze for
1 month. Refresh in a hot oven to
crisp them up, then continue from
step 8.

For the pastry
1 cup all-purpose flour
1 tsp sugar
a pinch of salt
¾ stick (¼ cup plus 2 tbsp) butter,
    plus extra for greasing
1 cup water
3 eggs

For the chocolate sauce
7 oz bittersweet chocolate, 60–70%
    cocoa solids, broken into pieces
½ cup heavy cream
½ cup milk
1 tsp vanilla paste or extract
a pinch of salt

For the filling
2 cups heavy cream
2 tbsp confectioners' sugar
½ tsp vanilla paste or extract

1

For the pastry, first sift the flour, sugar, and salt together onto a piece of parchment paper.

2

Put the butter and water in a medium pan. Heat over fairly low heat until the butter has completely melted. Once melted, increase the heat and bring the water to a rolling boil. Keep a wooden spoon on hand. With the pan still on the stove, and using the parchment paper like a chute, quickly pour the flour mixture into the pan, then grab the wooden spoon and start mixing it vigorously. Turn off the heat. It will seem weirdly lumpy at first, but keep beating. You need to add the flour soon after the water comes to a boil, to avoid letting too much evaporate.

3

After a short period of beating, the lumpy batter will transform into a shiny, thick smooth paste that comes away cleanly from the edge of the pan. Stop beating.

4

Spoon the paste onto a cold plate and spread it out with the wooden spoon. This helps to cool it quickly. When it's barely warm to the touch, move on to step 5.

5

Beat the eggs together in a measuring cup. Put the paste in a large bowl, then add the egg in small additions, beating until fully incorporated each time. The paste will get stiffer, then looser. You can do this with an electric mixer if you prefer. Stop adding egg when the mixture is smooth and silky, and falls in a smooth dollop from the spoon when shaken sharply. The paste can be chilled for up to a day at this point.

6

When ready to bake, preheat the oven to 425°F. Grease and line 2 large baking sheets with parchment paper. Spoon 18 heaping teaspoons pastry onto the sheets, aiming for walnut-sized balls. If you want to be neat, pipe the pastry onto the sheets using a ½-inch tip and a large pastry bag. Smooth any points with a wet finger.

7

Bake for 10 minutes at 425°F, then turn down the oven to 400°F and cook for 20 minutes, or until very crisp and golden brown. The pastry should hardly give at all when gently squeezed. It's best to bake in batches, but if you need to, bake 2 sheets at a time. Don't open the oven door to turn the sheets around until the pastry has risen well and is changing color, or they will deflate. Once cooked, cut each profiterole crosswise, but not all the way through, then bake for 5 minutes more. This lets the steam out from the centers and will help keep the pastry crisper for longer. Remove and let cool.

8

To make the sauce, chop the chocolate. Bring the cream and milk to a simmer, add the chocolate, vanilla, and salt, then remove from the heat and stir until smooth and silky. It can be made ahead and warmed gently when ready to serve.

9

Profiteroles are best filled shortly before serving, but you can fill them 2 hours ahead and store them in the fridge. Put the cream, sugar, and vanilla in a large bowl and whip until thickened, but not stiff. Spoon it generously into the cold profiteroles.

10

Pour the warm chocolate sauce over them to serve.

One-Crust Apple & Blackberry Pie

Preparation time: 25 minutes,
plus chilling (if making own pastry)
Baking time: 35–50 minutes
Serves 8

This is the most democratic of pies, and needs no special equipment. A simple, sturdy, but tender pastry crust holds the juicy contents inside (or you can use 12 oz store-bought dough). Try using rhubarb and strawberries or perhaps peaches and blueberries once you've got the hang of it.

For the basic sweet pie dough

1⅔ cups all-purpose flour,
    plus extra for rolling

¼ tsp salt

¼ cup cold vegetable shortening

½ stick plus 1 tbsp (¼ cup plus
    1 tbsp) cold butter

1 egg

2 tbsp sugar

For the filling

1 lb 7 oz tart, sweet apples
    (about 3–4)

1 lemon, or 1 tbsp lemon juice
    from a bottle

2 tbsp cornstarch

½ tsp ground cinnamon or nutmeg

½–1 cup blackberries, fresh or
    frozen and thawed (or other soft,
    sharp fruit)

½ cup sugar

2 tbsp semolina or fine cornmeal

1 tbsp butter

1 tbsp turbinado sugar

1
Make the pastry first. Sift the flour into a large bowl and add the salt. Cut the shortening and butter into cubes, then add to the bowl. Separate the egg and beat the yolk with 2 tablespoons water. Reserve the egg white for later on.

2
Rub the fat into the flour with your hands until the mixture resembles fine crumbs, then stir in the sugar. A food processor makes light work of this job, if you have one.

3
Splash the egg yolk and water over the rubbed-in mixture, then quickly work it in using a table knife until it comes together. If using a processor, process until the pastry comes together to a smooth ball. Try to avoid adding any more liquid, or mixing it too much once the dough starts to take shape. If the dough really won't come together, add 1 teaspoon more water. Some flours are drier than others, so the amount of liquid you need can vary.

4
If making by hand, knead the dough briefly to make a smooth ball. Whichever way you make it, shape the dough into a disk, wrap in plastic wrap, then chill for 30 minutes, or until firm but not rock hard, while you prepare the filling. Preheat the oven to 375°F. Put a baking sheet in the oven to heat up. This will provide a boost of heat to the bottom of the pastry, helping it to crisp.

5
Peel the apples, chop the flesh away from the cores in big chunks, then slice them thinly. Toss in a large bowl with 1 tbsp lemon juice, the cornstarch, spice, and berries. Don't add the sugar yet, as it can make the fruit a little wet by the time the pastry is ready.

6

Cut a large square of parchment paper and sprinkle it lightly with flour. Using a floured rolling pin, press ridges evenly across the pastry. Rotate the pastry and paper by a quarter turn and repeat. Do this until the pastry is about ½ inch thick. If any cracks appear at the edges, pinch them back together.

7

Roll the pastry out into a 12-inch round. Roll forwards and back, not side to side, and turn the pastry and paper a quarter turn every few rolls. This will help the pastry stretch without becoming tough.

8

Slide the pastry, still on its paper, onto a flat baking sheet. Sprinkle the cornmeal or semolina over the middle. Toss the sugar into the fruit, then mound it in the middle of the pastry, leaving a border of about 3 inches. Lightly beat the egg white with a fork, then brush it around the edges with a pastry brush.

9

Push the pastry up and around the fruit, pinching it here and there to make a sort of basket shape. If any cracks appear, just pinch the pastry together to re-seal. Dot the butter over the fruit. Brush the outside of the pastry with the egg white and scatter with turbinado sugar.

10

Slide the baking sheet on top of the preheated baking sheet. Bake for 35–40 minutes, or until golden and crisp and the apples are just tender. If they are not quite cooked but the pastry is, reduce the temperature to 350°F and give it 10 more minutes. Cool for at least 10 minutes to let the juices settle, then serve hot or warm with ice cream, cream, or custard.

Upside-Down Fruit Cake

Preparation time: 20 minutes,
plus cooling
Baking time: 55 minutes–1 hour
Makes 12 slices

I love the way that despite its glossy looks, this is a down-to-earth bake, ready to change with the seasons as they roll round. Cherries, apricots, peaches, apples, pears, even the classic pineapple will happily meld into the bottom of the rich almond sponge. Serve slightly warm with sour cream or crème fraiche, or a pitcher of custard if it's cold outside.

For the cake

2 sticks plus 2 tbsp (1 cup plus
   2 tbsp) soft butter, plus extra
   for greasing
1¼ packed cups light brown sugar
1 cup plus 2 tbsp all-purpose flour
2 tsp baking powder
¼ tsp salt
1 cup almond meal
½ cup sour cream or crème fraîche
4 eggs, room temperature
½ tsp almond extract

For the fruit

8–10 firmish ripe plums
4 tbsp light brown sugar

1
Preheat the oven to 350°F. Use a little butter to grease a 9-inch round springform pan, then line the base with parchment paper. Halve and pit the plums, then cut each half into 3 wedges. Toss them with 4 tablespoons light brown sugar.

2
Arrange the fruit in the bottom of the pan in neat rings, if you have time, or be more rustic. They must be in a single layer. Make sure you add all the sugar.

3
Put the butter in a mixing bowl with the dry ingredients, sour cream or crème fraîche, eggs, and almond extract.

4

Use an electric mixer to beat everything to a smooth, fairly thick cake batter.

5

Spoon the batter on top of the fruit, then smooth the top.

6

Bake for 55 minutes–1 hour, or until the cake is golden and has risen; a skewer should come out clean when inserted into the center. Run an icing spatula around the edge of the pan to loosen the cake, then let cool on a cooling rack.

7

Serve the cake warm. If you need to reheat it, cover it loosely with foil and let it warm through in a low oven for 15 minutes.

PEAR & CHOCOLATE CAKE
Toss 1 lb sliced just-ripe pears with the sugar. Add 3½ oz semi-sweet chocolate chips to the cake batter.

PINEAPPLE CAKE
Toss 1 lb pineapple chunks (drained if canned) with the sugar. For a really retro touch, poke glacé cherries here and there between the fruit.

SPICED APPLE CARAMEL CAKE
Toss 1 lb sliced, peeled apples with the sugar. Mix 2 teaspoons pumpkin pie spice in with the flour. Drizzle with ready-made caramel sauce or dulce de leche to serve.

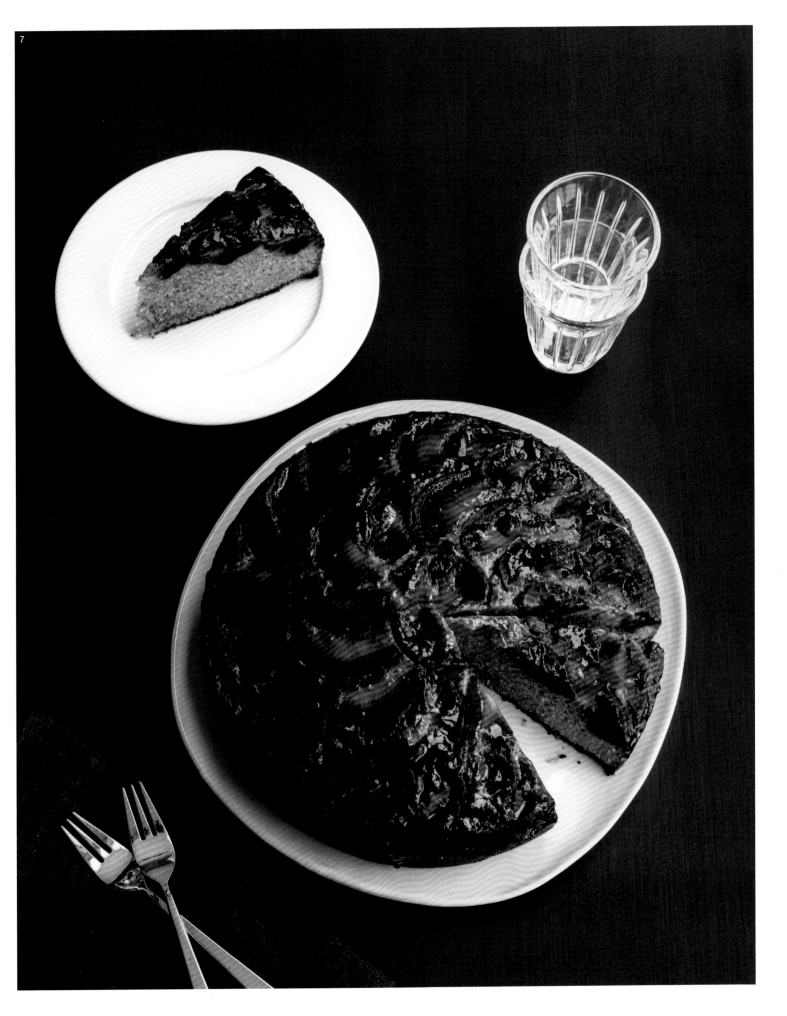

Classic Baked Cheesecake

Preparation time: 20 minutes,
plus chilling
Baking time: 55 minutes
Cuts into 12 generous slices,
more if you need it to

Creamy and cool, with a crisp base
with just a hint of ginger, this baked
cheesecake is sweet but not cloying.
The cooling time is all-important,
so make this the last thing you do
in the kitchen on the day you make
it. Serve with seasonal fruit, or pale
and interesting, all by itself.

For the base

1 stick (½ cup) soft butter

9 oz Graham crackers or
    digestive cookies

2 tbsp superfine sugar

½ tsp ground ginger (optional)

For the filling

2 lb full-fat cream cheese,
    at room temperature

1 cup superfine sugar

1 tbsp cornstarch

1 vanilla bean or 1 tsp vanilla paste

1 lemon

5 eggs, room temperature

1 cup full-fat crème fraîche
    (or use sour cream)

1

Preheat the oven to 400°F. Melt the butter in a medium pan, then use a little to grease a 9-inch round springform pan. Line the base with a circle of parchment paper. Crush the crackers until fine and sandy. You can do this by putting them in a strong plastic food storage bag, squishing out the air, then whacking them with a rolling pin. Or use a food processor, as I have here.

2

Mix the melted butter, 2 tablespoons sugar, and the ginger (if using) into the crumbs, until evenly blended and rather like wet sand. Press into the base of the pan, spreading firmly with the back of a spoon, until evenly spread.

3

Put the pan on a baking sheet, then bake for 10 minutes until golden. Let cool.

4

To make the filling, put the cream cheese and sugar in a large bowl, then sift the cornstarch over it. If using a vanilla bean, split it lengthwise and scrape out the seeds. Finely grate the zest from the lemon, and add the vanilla and lemon zest to the bowl. Using a spatula, beat until smooth. A spatula is better than a whisk here because you don't want to beat in too much air, which can cause cracks.

5

Separate 2 of the eggs (see page 127), saving the whites for another time. Beat the 3 whole eggs and 2 yolks into the cheese mixture one by one, until very smooth.

6

Finish by beating in ½ cup crème fraîche or sour cream. Pour the mixture onto the crumb crust, then level the top.

WHAT IS CRÈME FRAÎCHE?
Easily found in Europe, and now becoming more popular in the US, this cultured cream is thick, rich, and fantastic for baking. It has a sour flavor but is thicker and creamier than regular sour cream. Its slightly higher fat content makes for a very good cheesecake.

7

Bake for 10 minutes, then turn the oven down to 300°F and bake for another 45 minutes, or until the center wobbles slightly as you jiggle the pan, and the top has turned very pale gold at the edges. Check the cake after two thirds of the baking time and give it a turn if needed. When it's ready, loosen the edge of the cake from the pan using an icing spatula, then return to the turned-off oven and let it cool in the oven with the door ajar for 1 hour. Remove and let cool to room temperature for a couple of hours, then chill overnight.

8

For optimal creaminess, take the cheesecake from the fridge half an hour before you want to eat it. Smooth the rest of the crème fraîche over the top, then serve.

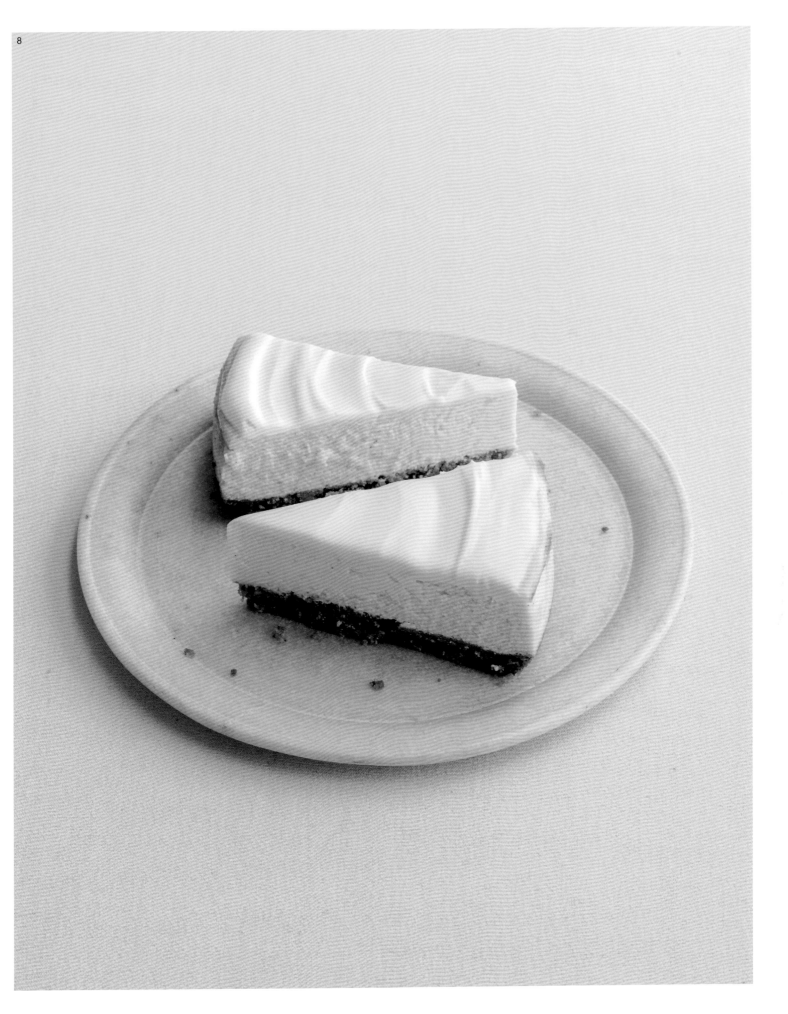

Mint-Chocolate Macarons

Preparation time: 25 minutes,
plus drying and settling time
Baking time: 12 minutes per batch
Makes 18–20 sandwiched macarons

Anyone can make homemade
macarons—with just a few pieces
of kitchen equipment, they're
more of a pleasure than a challenge,
and make a special after-dinner bite
or a perfect gift. They need time to
dry and set, so allow plenty of time.

For the basic macaron batter

1 cup almond meal

¾ cup plus 1 tbsp confectioners'
    sugar

3 egg whites

a pinch of salt

½ cup superfine sugar

green food coloring gel (optional)

For the mint-chocolate filling

3½ oz bittersweet chocolate,
    either 60 or 70% cocoa solids

½ tsp mint extract

½ cup heavy cream

1

Prepare 2 heavy baking sheets: line them with nonstick parchment paper, then draw 20 circles onto each sheet, allowing about 1 inch around each circle. I use an egg cup of 1¾-inch diameter, but a small pastry cutter or an upturned shot glass should be about right too. Fit a pastry bag with a ½-inch plain tip.

WHICH BAKING SHEET?
Dark, heavy, metal baking sheets give better results than lighter silver ones, creating more perfectly Parisian "feet" (a little skirt of bubbles) on the bottom of the macarons. Use your sturdiest baking sheet or pan.

2

Put the almond meal and confectioners' sugar in the bowl of a food processor and pulse until the almonds are very fine—about 30 seconds. I find that the sugar sinks to the bottom of the bowl, so after 15 seconds or so, give everything a stir and process again. Sift the mixture and discard any larger pieces of almond that remain.

3

Separate the eggs and measure the whites. You will need exactly ⅓ cup plus 1 tablespoon. Then, in a very clean large bowl and using an electric mixer, beat the egg whites with the salt until stiff, but not dry or fluffy around the edges.

4

Add 1 tablespoon of the superfine sugar, then beat again until the mixture returns to stiff peaks. Do this repeatedly until all the sugar has been used, and you have a thick, glossy bowl of meringue that looks rather like shaving cream.

5

Add a few dabs of of the food coloring, if using, and whisk again until evenly green. Food colorings go a long way and you can always add more, so go easy to begin with until you reach the color you want.

6

Fold the sifted almond and sugar mixture into the meringue. If at this point it is still very thick and fluffy, the macarons can turn out a little rougher-looking on the top when baked. If this is the case, break the meringue rules and beat the mixture a little with a spatula until it loosens ever so slightly. Transfer half the mixture to the pastry bag, taking care not to create too many pockets of air.

PIPING KNOW-HOW
Filling a pastry bag is much easier if you first open the bag out over your left hand if you are right handed (or vice versa), or over a tall glass or jam jar. You can then fill the bag, going no more than half full, before flipping the top of the bag back over and twisting the top to create the pressure needed to pipe.

7

Before you pipe, be sure to turn the paper over to avoid having pencil marks on the bottom of your macarons. Secure the paper to the baking sheets with a small dot of the meringue at either end. Pipe the mixture onto the marked circles, keeping the bag upright, starting in the middle of the circle, and then squeezing with an even pressure. Let the batter ooze out in one continuous flow until it almost reaches the pencil lines, then stop squeezing and lift the tip away. Gently press any points down with your finger (don't wet it), if you need to. You should get between 36 and 40 circles.

8

Let the macarons dry for 1 hour, to let a skin form over the top. It's best if you don't cook anything else steamy in the kitchen at the same time. The batter should not stick to your finger when touched lightly. Preheat the oven to 325°F.

9

Bake the macarons, one sheet at a time, for 12 minutes, or until they have risen on little bubbly platforms, and look shiny on top. Try to avoid letting them turn golden; turn the sheet halfway through if they look uneven. Once cooked, carefully pull the paper, complete with macarons, off the baking sheet and let cool on a flat work surface.

10

To make the filling, chop the chocolate and put it in a bowl with the mint extract. Bring the cream to a boil in a small pan, then pour this over the chocolate. Allow to melt, stirring every now and again, until smooth.

11

When the ganache is cool, thick and glossy, sandwich the macarons together. Spoon about 1 teaspoon of the ganache on top of the flat sides of half of the macarons. Gently sandwich with the other halves. The chocolate will ooze out to the edges.

12

Let the filling set completely. Keep the macarons in a cool place until serving.

PISTACHIO MACARONS
Grind ½ cup shelled pistachios in the processor, then measure ½ cup pistachio meal. Process with ½ cup almond meal and the confectioners' sugar. Sandwich with chocolate ganache, leaving out the mint extract.

RASPBERRY MACARONS
Color the mixture with pink food coloring. Sandwich the macarons with 1 teaspoon best-quality raspberry jam.

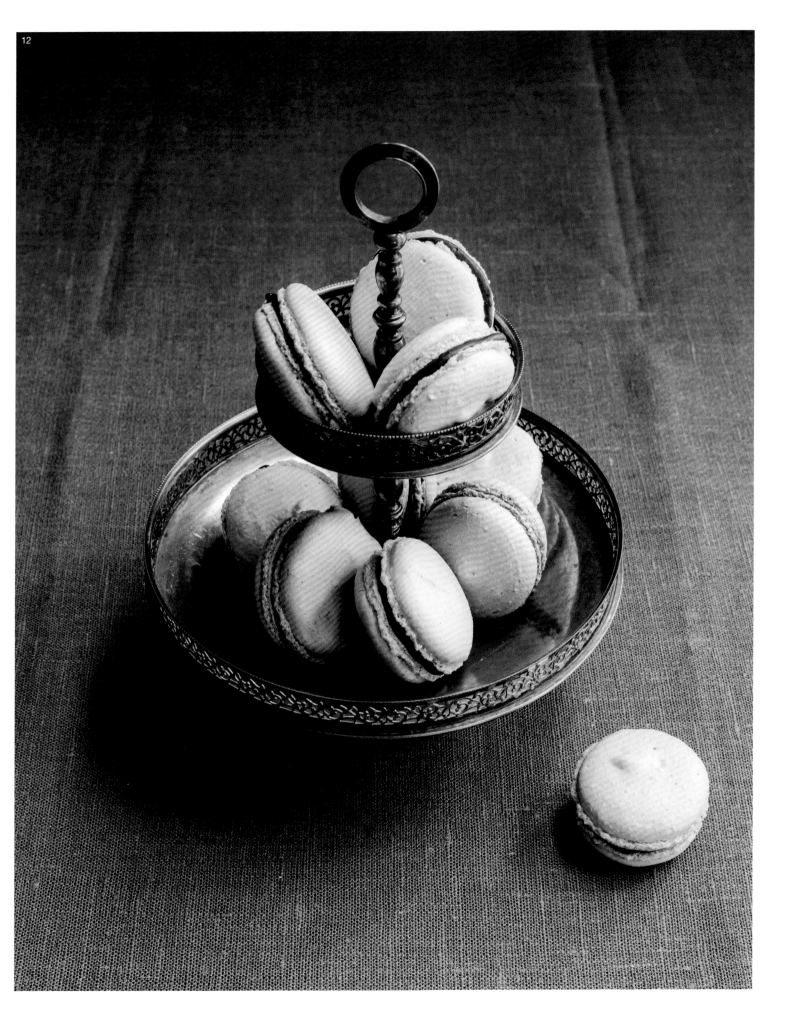

Pistachio & Fig Biscotti

Preparation time: 20 minutes,
plus cooling
Baking time: 1 hour
Makes about 36 biscotti

It's easy to make your own elegant
biscotti, baked twice for just the
right crunch, ready for dunking into
coffee or sweet dessert wine after
dinner, or crumbling over ice cream.
I've chosen figs and pistachio, for
flavor and their graphic, colorful
cross-section, but any combination
of dried fruit and nuts will work
brilliantly.

2 tbsp olive oil, plus a little extra
   for greasing
4 oz soft dried figs
   (or other dried fruit)
1 cup sugar
3 eggs, room temperature
2⅓ cups all-purpose flour,
   plus extra for rolling
1 tsp baking powder
½ tsp salt
1 orange
scant cup shelled pistachios,
   almonds or hazelnuts

1
Grease then line a large baking sheet with parchment paper. Preheat the oven to 350°F. Snip or cut the figs into small pieces.

2
Put the sugar and eggs in a large bowl, then whisk for a minute or so with a hand whisk, just until the mixture feels frothy and a little more resistant as you beat. Whisk in the oil.

3
Mix the flour, baking powder, and salt, then sift them over the egg mixture. Fold together to make a dough. Finely grate the zest from the orange, then work it into the dough along with the nuts and figs, using a spatula.

4
Scatter some flour on the work surface and turn the dough out onto it. Split the dough into 2 equal balls, dust each one (and your hands) with a little flour, then shape into an 8–10-inch sausage. The dough is quite soft, so be gentle with it, and pat it into shape rather than squeezing it too much. Lift it onto the prepared baking sheet.

5

Bake for 30 minutes, or until it has risen and turned pale golden. Let cool, and in the meantime turn the oven down to 325°F.

6

When the dough is firm and cool enough to handle, transfer the biscotti to a board and cut into ½-inch slices. Use a serrated knife and sawing action, as the dough is quite sturdy by this point. Spread the cookies over the baking sheet in a single layer. Use a second sheet if you want to bake all the cookies at once.

GETTING AHEAD
The half-baked biscotti can be frozen at this point and baked from frozen when needed. Allow a few more minutes of baking time.

7

Return the biscotti to the oven and bake for another 30 minutes, turning them over halfway through, until dry, crisp, and just golden. If you are baking 2 sheets at once, swap their shelf positions half way through cooking too.

8

Cool the biscotti on a rack, then pack in an airtight container until serving. They will last up to 2 weeks.

SPICED PECAN-CRANBERRY BISCOTTI
Sift 2 teaspoons pumpkin pie spice into the flour. Replace the pistachios and figs with pecans and cranberries.

ANISE & ALMOND BISCOTTI
Work in whole blanched almonds instead of the pistachios, and add 1 teaspoon lightly crushed anise or fennel seeds.

Salted Caramel Shortbread Bites

Preparation time: 45 minutes,
plus setting
Baking time: 25–30 minutes
Makes 36 small cubes

If you're a fan of the salt and
caramel combination but haven't
tried it at home yet, this is a delicious
way to experiment. The recipe is
a twist on millionaire's shortbread,
a classic British childhood favorite
of mine. It's now all grown up, and
perfect as a bite after dinner.

For the base

1 stick (½ cup) soft butter, plus
   extra for greasing
¼ cup sugar
a pinch of flaky sea salt
½ tsp vanilla extract
1 cup plus 2 tbsp all-purpose flour

For the caramel

1 stick (½ cup) butter
1 packed cup dark brown sugar
¼ cup golden syrup, such as Lyle's,
   or corn syrup
½ tsp flaky sea salt
14-oz can full-fat condensed milk

For the topping

7 oz bittersweet chocolate,
   70% cocoa solids
1 tbsp vegetable or sunflower oil
½ tsp flaky sea salt

1
Lightly grease a 9-inch square baking pan, then line with parchment paper. Make the base first. Put the butter in a large bowl and beat well with a wooden spoon or an electric mixer until creamy and very pale. Add the sugar, salt, and vanilla and beat again until even paler.

2
Sift the flour over the creamed butter and sugar. Using a spatula, gently work the flour into the mixture to make an evenly blended dough that starts to clump together.

3
Press the dough into the prepared pan, then level and smooth it with the back of a spoon. Prick it all over with a fork, then chill for 10 minutes, or longer if you like, until firm. Meanwhile, preheat the oven to 325°F.

4
Bake for 25–30 minutes, or until the shortbread is golden all over. Let cool completely.

QUICK SHORTCUT
If you prefer, buy 14 oz ready-made, all-butter shortbread cookies. Crush them finely, then stir in 4 tablespoons melted butter until evenly blended. Press into the pan, bake for 15 minutes, or until golden, then continue with the recipe.

5
Now for the caramel. Melt the butter, sugar, syrup, and salt together gently in a pan, then stir in the condensed milk.

6

Bring the caramel to a simmer, stirring constantly with a spatula, and let it bubble for 4 minutes, or until it thickens and smells like creamy toffee. It should be thick enough for the spatula to leave a trail in the caramel for a few seconds. Don't leave the pan or stop stirring during this step, as it can easily burn on the base.

7

Pour the caramel over the shortbread, then let cool completely.

8

Once the caramel has set and cooled, it's time to finish the layers. Melt the chocolate either over a pan of water or in the microwave (see page 119), stir in the oil, then pour this over the caramel. Sprinkle with the salt and let set at room temperature, or in the fridge if it's a hot day. The oil helps stop the chocolate setting too hard, which can make it difficult to cut.

9

When the chocolate is just set, mark it into squares (I use a ruler to get the lines perfectly straight), then chill until completely firm.

10

Cut into cubes to serve. For a really clean finish, wipe the blade of your knife with a slightly damp cloth between each slicing. Store in an airtight container for up to 3 days.

MILLIONAIRE'S SHORTBREAD
To make the British classic millionaire's shortbread, simply reduce the salt to a pinch in the caramel, and omit it from the top too.

What to Bake

If you're still not sure what to bake for a particular occasion or need, how about a few of these suggestions?

No time to bake?
Fruity Cupcakes, 26
Favorite Jelly Roll, 38
Vanilla Sponge Cake
   (using all-in-one method), 46
Chocolate & Nut Banana Bread, 50
Malted Milk Chocolate
   Birthday Cake, 64
Carrot Cake with Cream Cheese
   Frosting (as cupcakes), 92
Skinny Blueberry Muffins, 104

Bake-sale bestsellers
Golden Citrus Drizzle Cake, 22
Malted Milk Chocolate Birthday
   Cake (without the candles), 64
Cherry-Almond Streusel Slice, 88
Buttermilk Pound Cake
   (lemon flavor), 30
Carrot Cake with Cream
   Cheese Frosting (whole or
   as cupcakes), 92
Caramel & Walnut Coffee Cake, 110
Jaffa Marble Loaf, 84

Baking with children
Peanut Butter Cookies, 34
Fruity Cupcakes, 26
Iced Gingerbread Cookies, 42
Lemon & Raisin Pancakes, 52
Favorite Jelly Roll, 38
Skinny Blueberry Muffins, 104
Red Velvet Whoopie Pies
   (banoffee variation), 164

Children's birthday parties
Rocky Road, 56
Fruity Cupcakes, 26
Malted Milk Chocolate
   Birthday Cake, 64
Peanut Butter Cookies
   or Seriously Chocolatey
   Cookies (as ice-cream
   sandwiches), 34/118

Bake ahead & freeze
Jaffa Marble Loaf, 84

Vanilla Sponge Cake, 46
Chocolate Fudge Layer Cake, 134
Seriously Chocolatey Cookies, 118
Peanut Butter Cookies, 34
Cranberry Stollen, 182

Picnics & camping
Blueberry-Cinnamon
   Crumb Cake, 114
Golden Citrus Drizzle Cake, 22
Rocky Road, 56
Whole Orange & Almond Cake, 202
Salted Caramel Shortbread Bites, 232
Jaffa Marble Loaf, 84
Buttermilk Pound Cake, 30
Chocolate & Nut Banana Bread, 50

Baby shower
Frosted Cupcakes (use baby blue
   and pink or yellow colouring), 160
Mint-Chocolate Macarons
   (raspberry variation), 22
Fudgy Cheesecake Brownies, 96
Linzer Cookies (sandwiched
   with lemon curd), 138

Wedding, anniversary or formal party
Vanilla Celebration Cake, 168
Festive Fruit Cake, 176
Frosted Cupcakes, 160
Chocolate Fudge Layer Cake, 134

Classic English afternoon tea party
Classic Crusty Bread (made
   into cucumber sandwiches), 68
Vanilla Fruit Scones (with cream
   and jam), 60
Classic Shortbread, 76
Tart au Citron (cut into
   small pieces), 192

Valentine's Day
Red Velvet Whoopie Pies, 164
Fudgy Cheesecake Brownies
   (swirl the topping in heart shapes), 96
Mint-Chocolate Macarons
   (raspberry variation), 222
Classic Shortbread
   (lavender variation), 76

Easter
Chocolate Fudge Layer Cake
   (topped with chocolate eggs), 134

Chocolate Hazelnut Log (decorate
   with chicks, chocolate eggs
   and spring flowers), 172
Festive Fruit Cake, 176

Mother's Day
Blueberry-Cinnamon
   Crumb Cake, 114
Coconut Layer Cake, 142
Classic Baked Cheesecake, 218
Lemon-Glazed Ginger Cake, 100
Angel Cake with Berries, 152
Vanilla Celebration Cake, 168
Chocolate Fudge Layer Cake, 134
Strawberry Meringue Cake, 198

Fourth of July/Labor Day
Angel Cake with Berries, 152
Malted Milk Chocolate
   Birthday Cake (with red,
   white, and blue candies), 64
Red Velvet Whoopie Pies, 164

Halloween
Red Velvet Whoopie Pies
   (pumpkin variation), 164
Malted Milk Chocolate Birthday
   Cake (graveyard variation), 64
Easy Baked Doughnuts, 126
Linzer Cookies (vampire-style;
   puncture two holes in the top
   cookies to let the jam
   ooze through), 138

Thanksgiving
Sticky Pear & Pecan
   Toffee Cake, 156
Pumpkin Pie, 148
Red Velvet Whoopie Pies
   (pumpkin variation), 164
Carrot Cake with Cream
   Cheese Frosting, 92
Upside-Down Fruit Cake
   (apple caramel variation), 214

Christmas
Festive Fruit Cake, 176
Cranberry Stollen, 182
Sticky Pear & Pecan Toffee Cake, 156
Chocolate Hazelnut Log, 172
Linzer Cookies, 138
Pistachio & Fig Biscotti (spiced
   pecan cranberry variation), 228

Index

With thanks

I couldn't have made this book without the help and support from these wonderful people. For the photos, Liz and Max Haarala Hamilton, thank you for all your spirit, creativity, and the gorgeous shots, and Ruth Carruthers for lightening their load. Thanks also to my assistants Sophie Austen-Smith, Hannah Sherwood, and Lucy Campbell for keeping the cakes a-coming, and not to forget Teresa Coen and my wonderful mum Linda for stepping in and saving the day.

Thanks to Leslie Hutchings for your advice and to my heroic recipe testers, Mum (again), Pip Bennett, Helen Barker-Benfield, Germaine McBride, Lucy Campbell, Pauline Copestake, Catherine Gardner, Sarah Goss, and Emma Henry for baking my recipes in your own kitchens.

To the all of the Phaidon team, but most especially Emma Robertson for kicking this whole thing off, and to Laura Gladwin for taking it through to the finish line. Thanks to Kerry Lemon for her brilliant, stand-out illustrations, and Ana Minguez for her careful design work. In the US, thanks to Cindi Kruth for testing the recipes with such diligence, and to Karen Berman for her keen eye on the proofs. Grateful thanks to Magimix UK for help with equipment.

Finally, to Ross, for all your belief and support, and all our friends, family, and neighbors, who've eaten the contents of this book three times over. We made this together, everyone; thank you from the bottom of my heart.

Note on the recipes

Some recipes include raw or very lightly cooked eggs. These should be avoided by the elderly, infants, pregnant women, convalescents, and anyone with an impaired immune system.

Phaidon Press Inc.
65 Bleecker Street
New York, NY 10012

www.phaidon.com

© 2014 Phaidon Press Limited

ISBN 978 0 7148 6865 3

A CIP catalogue record is available from the British Library.

Commissioning Editor: Emma Robertson
Project Editor: Laura Gladwin
Production Controller: Mandy Mackie

Photographs by Liz and Max Haarala Hamilton
Illustrations by Kerry Lemon
Design concept by SML Office
Layout by Ana Minguez

Printed in China